Ed Glin

T0270279

111 Places in Oxford That You Shouldn't Miss

Photographs by David Taylor

emons:

For Katy

Layout: Eva Kraskes, based on a design
by Lübbeke | Naumann | Thoben
Maps: altancicek.design, www.altancicek.de
Basic cartographical information from Openstreetmap,
© OpenStreetMap-Mitwirkende, OdbL
Editing: Ros Horton
Printing and binding: Grafisches Centrum Cuno, Calbe
Printed in Germany 2023
ISBN 978-3-7408-1990-3
First edition

Guidebooks for Locals & Experienced Travellers
Join us in uncovering new places around the world at
www.111places.com

Foreword

Oxford is the home of superlatives. Is it really the finest city in the world as Keats claimed 200 years ago? Was W. B. Yeats right when he wondered how anyone in Oxford did anything but 'dream and remember; the place is so beautiful. One almost expects the people to sing instead of speaking'?

Yes, everything you've read about Oxford, all the compliments you've heard, are true. The world's most famous university city is immediately, obviously beautiful, for it is filled with the most heart-warming architecture. College buildings wrought from classy Cotswold stone replete with Classical embellishments. Theatres and halls created by the greatest of architects: Christopher Wren, Nicholas Hawksmoor, William Butterfield. A city built on the love of learning, alma mater to many of the greatest figures in English history: John Wycliffe, William Tyndale, Shelley, John Ruskin, Graham Greene, Harold Wilson, defined in the most glorious of literature: *Jude the Obscure*, *Brideshead Revisited*, John Betjeman's poems.

Head to Carfax, the centre of Oxford, and soak in the heady mix of historical romance and urban pleasure. Then strike off east along High Street, described by Nikolaus Pevsner, the leading architectural critic, as 'one of the world's great streets'. College after college, grand shop after grand shop, the cream of the nation's youth bursting with intellectual rigour, tourists from afar agog at the excitement and extravagance.

Later, return to Carfax to sidle south along St Aldate's to Christ Church Meadow, the most glorious example of *rus in urbe* in Britain, which inspired the dreams of Alice in Wonderland. Or head to the pubs of St Giles and sup where Tolkien and C. S. Lewis debated, and Philip Larkin mused. Then stroll along its picturesque streams and rivers and head into a countryside of gentle rolling hills and charming villages. You won't want to leave.

111 Places

1 The Alice Shop

A sheep in sheep's clothing

In mid-Victorian times, this was the shop where the children of Henry Liddell, the Dean of Christ Church, used to buy their sweetmeats. The Dean's colleague was the Revd Charles Lutwidge Dodgson, better known as Lewis Carroll, so it's only fitting that this 15th-century house is now the Alice Shop, purveyors of all things *Alice in Wonderland* – Alician tea bags, postcards, magnets, thimbles, stuffed toys – the lot.

How did Charles Lutwidge Dodgson change his name? First he Latinised Charles Lutwidge to Carolus Ludovicus, then he reversed the order and de-Latinised it to Lewis Carroll. The fantastical author featured these premises as the Old Sheep Shop in *Through the Looking-Glass* (1871). One of John Tenniel's original illustrations shows the inside, and Chapter 5, 'Wool and Water', has the shop owned by a sheep, as in the following encounter. 'Was it really a sheep that was sitting on the other side of the counter?… She was in a little dark shop, leaning with her elbows on the counter, and opposite to her was an old Sheep, sitting in an arm-chair knitting, and every now and then leaving off to look at her through a great pair of spectacles.'

Later, the shop itself vanishes, and Alice finds herself outside with the sheep in a boat, holding a pair of knitting needles, which turn into oars. The sheep sells Alice an egg, which turns into Humpty Dumpty, leaving Alice to announce: 'Well, this is the very queerest shop I ever saw!'

It was appropriate that the shop had a watery surreal transformation in the story, for in real life the building was prone to flooding, thanks to the underground Trill Mill Stream. The building was saved 100 years ago by a Dr Gunther of Magdalen College who wrote to *The Times* when the houses opposite were being demolished. It sold groceries through to the 1960s when *Alice in Wonderland* memorabilia began to show up on its shelves.

Address 83 St Aldate's OX1 1RA, +44 (0)1865 240338, www.aliceinwonderlandshop.com |
Getting there Bus 1, 5 or 5A; Oxford Station is 10 minutes to the west | Hours Daily
10.30am–5pm | Tip Head across Christ Church Meadow to – where else but the Mad
Hatter venue on Iffley Road, for victuals that probably won't reduce you to one foot six.

2   Another Time II
Don't look now

He stands guard over Broad Street in the heart of Oxford University. He might be making sure than any neophyte Boris Johnsons or Rees-Moggies behave themselves. He is *Another Time II*, a statue of a nude man standing on the roof of Blackwell's Art and Poster shop at the corner with Turl Street, frightening passers-by who happen to look up.

Another Time II stands seven feet in his metallic shoes and weighs half a tonne. He is the work of master sculptor Antony Gormley, of *Angel of the North* fame, who has explained that the figure was inspired by his own physique. No one knows how *Another Time II* got up there in 2009, well, apart from the 20 workmen who hoisted him, and the crowd that watched the bursar of nearby Exeter College try to align him with Martyrs' Cross in the middle of the road. As Gormley has explained, 'The casual passer-by will ask, "What is that naked iron bloke doing up there?", for which I hope there will never be a single satisfactory answer… It is separated from shelter of the architecture that might otherwise contain it'.

Exeter College was thrilled when an anonymous benefactor provided the funds to secure the figure. A spokesman explained that 'it is important for the visibility of the sculpture to be positioned close to the parapet of the building'. However, the statue did not arrive without controversy. Ten days before the unveiling, councillors announced that he didn't have planning permission. Fortunately, the Mayoress allowed the event to go ahead.

But beware. *Another Time II* is one of a series. Already similar pieces elsewhere have sparked anxious calls to the police fearing someone was about to throw themselves off a building. When rain and water dripped off one of Gormley's London figures onto a passer-by, she contacted the police to report that someone standing on a building had urinated on her. Check your roofs, folks.

Address 27 Broad Street OX1 3BS | Getting there Bus 6 or 13; Broad Street is a 10-minute walk east from Oxford Station | Hours Accessible 24 hours | Tip Underneath yer man is Blackwell's well-stocked art and poster shop.

3 — Anthony Blanche's Fountain
'Rococo, dear boy'

In Oxford's greatest novel, Evelyn Waugh's *Brideshead Revisited* (1945), the aesthete Anthony Blanche is accosted by some rough types who try to toss him into the Mercury fountain in the Tom Quad of Christ Church. Nonplussed, he tells the novel's narrator, Charles Ryder, how enthusiastic he had been, announcing to his tor-mentors: 'Nothing could give me keener pleasure than to be manhan-dled by you meaty boys.' This stumps them and he climbs in himself. 'You heard about [the students'] treatment of me on Thursday? It was too naughty. Luckily I was wearing my oldest pyjamas or I might have been seriously cross.'

Waugh was simply recognising a traditional jape whereby 'Hearties' (sporty students) would throw 'Aesthetes' (artistic students) into the water. Nowadays, the rag can lead to a heavy fine, for the pond con-tains large koi carp donated by the Empress of Japan in 2007. This is the second Mercury fountain and features a base by Sir Edwin Lutyens. The first was a fountain in the form of a serpent and fea-tured a lead-gilt globe. It was not decorative, but an important source of water at a time of fears about fires. Unfortunately, it was destroyed by the 14th Earl of Derby, later Tory PM three times, who tore down the lead and bronze centrepieces in a Johnsonian bout of high japes in 1817. At least the head of Mercury was saved and is now in the college library. A later Tory prime minister, Lord Salisbury, infiltrated the Hearties, tipped off his friends about the time of a planned raid, and arranged a counter-ambush.

The grandeur and scale of Tom Quad is down to Thomas Wolsey, Henry VIII's Archbishop of York and Lord Chancellor, who believed Latin, Greek and philosophy should be taught alongside theology and scripture. In 1524, the Pope gave Wolsey permission to dissolve the monastery of St Frideswide's that stood here and convert the site into a college.

Address St Aldate's OX1 1DP | Getting there Bus 1, 5 or 5A; Oxford Station is 10 minutes to the west | Hours Only on official college tours, pre-booked online or in the Visitor Centre on the day | Tip Head south and stay out of the water with a safer drink at The Head of the River pub to the south.

4 Aston Martin Museum
The car's Bond's – James Bond's

If you were going to open a museum dedicated to James Bond's favourite car, the epitome of style, luxury and performance, the most obvious place might not be a 15th-century barn, built by the monks of Dorchester Abbey, in what Autoblog have called 'the periphery of the exurbs of nowhere on a dirt road'. Or maybe such an anomaly is just the thing you might find in a wacky new 007 film.

The collection contains the official archives of the Aston Martin Lagonda company and those of the Aston Martin owners' club. The museum has received a host of donations over the years, including toy cars, trophies and posters. More importantly, the museum contains the 1921 A 3, the oldest existing Aston Martin remaining, which won the Kop Hill climb in 1922. It was bought at an auction in 2000, following which Sheikh Nasser of Kuwait then paid to restore it. The 1934 Ulster BLB 684 is a bit of a tricky beast. It has the clutch in the centre, and the brake and accelerator on either side.

Aston Martin was begun by Lionel Martin and Robert Bamford, who sold Singer cars in London and decided to build a racing car in their West London workshop. They got the name because they raced cars in the Aston Hinton Hill climb. Their first car was registered in 1915 and earned the nickname the 'Coal Scuttle'. Celebrity status came when the DB5 was used in the 1964 James Bond film *Goldfinger*. The make has been a regular since, and of course they are often fitted with the kind of gadgets you don't see in the Sainsbury's car park, such as a water cannon and room for a jetpack. Just watch any James Bond film.

Nowadays it's all about the hyper car, the Aston Martin Valkyrie, and the models created at the state-of-the-art factory in Gaydon, Warwickshire. If you're lucky, you might see one being driven by modern day celebs who love the make, including David Beckham, Rafael Nadal and Jason Statham.

Address Off Dorchester Road, Drayton St Leonard, Wallingford OX10 7BG, +44 (0)1865 400414, www.amht.org.uk | Getting there Head to Drayton St Leonard. The barn is near the junction of Dorchester Road and High Street. | Hours Daily 10am–4pm, but the museum is open only to pre-booked visitors, so contact them via the website | Tip No trip to the area would be complete without a period of reflection in Dorchester Abbey, home of nearly 1,400 years of Christianity.

5 Beating the Bounds
The wall that protects the city from invaders

In case any visiting armies or aliens wish to attack Oxford, the old walls on Queen's Lane will sort of protect the city from invaders. And just so that nobody forgets, every three years the Lord Mayor of Oxford joins forces with the college's governing body to stroll through town, repelling marauders, by 'beating the bounds' – inspecting the walls and marking the boundary stones to make sure they're doing their job. No stone is left unturned as participants walk up ladders and climb scaffolding while the vicar beats the stones with willow wands shouting: 'Mark, mark, mark!'

The event has taken place on Ascension Day, the 40th day after Easter, since 1428. Occasionally the bound beaters come across a problem. When they recently headed for the fashion shop Zara to beat the stone in a store area known as the 'Beat the Bounds room', they discovered that the shop was now TK Maxx, and were obstructed by two burly security guards. Following some hasty negotiations, the Revd Anthony Buckley persuaded the guards to let them in round the back, after which they hit the stone and left, the staff astounded.

The last stop for Beating the Bounds is at Lincoln College, where at lunchtime the connecting door with Brasenose College is opened to allow in members of the latter. This tradition dates back to a legend that a Brasenose man was pursued by a town mob and murdered at the gates of Lincoln. It became the custom for Lincoln to taint the beer with ground ivy to discourage Brasenose students from partaking of too much hospitality.

By the walls is New College, best known as Alma Mater to the Revd William Spooner, the bizarre late 19th-century cleric. Spooner was notorious for mixing up syllables, the classic being: 'You have hissed all my mystery lectures and were caught fighting a liar in the quad. You have tasted two whole worms and will leave by the next town drain'.

Address Queen's Lane OX1 4AR | Getting there Bus 3, 3A, 8 or 10; a 20-minute walk from Oxford Station | Hours Accessible 24 hours | Tip Check out the nearby deconsecrated church of St Peter-in-the-East and the statue of the popular 13th-century preacher St Edmund in the churchyard.

6 Best Designed College
Nuffield still motoring along

Have you ever wondered how the various Oxford colleges came into being… maybe from the largesse of a legendary academic or philanthropic nobleman, maybe investment by an inspired intellectual? Well, in the case of Nuffield College, easily identifiable by its simple, unadorned, lofty tower set half-way between Oxford Station and Carfax, it boils down to the Bullnose car, the Morris Minor and some of the most stylish motors of the 20th century.

Nuffield College was founded in 1937 through the wealth of Lord Nuffield. He was born in 1877 as William Morris (no relation to the great Victorian philanthropist of the same name), and took advantage of the boom in bicycling and the invention of the motor car to open a garage near Magdalen College at the end of the 19th century. Morris cars were aimed at the middle classes and known for their quality. After the Great War, the company dominated the British car industry, although its status fell in the 1970s when it acquired the doomed British Leyland.

Nuffield built this college on land around the Oxford Canal basin that was a slum. Nuffield College now motors along successfully, specialising in social sciences, economics, politics and sociology. It was the first to accept both men and women, co-ed from the start, and by 2013 was the wealthiest educational institution per student in the world. Famous alumni include long-standing late 20th-century Labour MP Austin Mitchell, who was never off the telly, Mark Carney, former Governor of the Bank of England, and the political scientist John Curtice. In recent years, the billionaire businessman and philanthropist George Soros has pledged several millions to fund a new economics institute.

But was Lord Nuffield happy about the success of the college? No. In a famous diatribe, he denounced the college as 'that bloody Kremlin where left-wingers study at my expense'.

Address New Road OX1 1NF, +44 (0)1865 278500, www.nuffield.ox.ac.uk | Getting there Bus 4A; Oxford Station is nearby | Hours Open for visitors Mon–Fri 9am–5pm | Tip Explore the nearby Worcester Street area with its canal, tributaries and disappearing traces of the old waterside industries.

7 _ Bill Clinton's Address

Where he didn't inhale – but someone did

Bill Clinton was president of America from 1993 till 2001. It was a time when US leaders could string a couple of sentences together. He arrived in Oxford as a Rhodes Scholar in 1968 with opposition to the Vietnam War, one of the main things on the minds of all Americans, and soon moved into this charming Jericho terraced house.

Contemporaries continue to gush about their Clintonian experiences. Katherine Gieve, who became a solicitor in London, later recalled how 'Bill was thinking about people. He made a relationship between abstract ideas and the meaning of people's experiences'. Oh dear. The novelist Sara Maitland recalled how 'Bill and his housemate, Frank Aller, took me to a pub in Walton Street in the summer term of 1969 and talked to me about the Vietnam War. When Frank began to describe the napalming of civilians I began to cry. Bill said that feeling bad wasn't good enough. That was the first time I encountered the idea that liberal sensitivities weren't enough and you had to do something about such things'. Tragically Aller, also a Rhodes Scholar, committed suicide in 1971, for reasons that may have been related to dodging the draft.

Yet thanks to populist tabloid sensationalist journalism, the only thing anyone wants to hear about regarding the Pres' Oxford sojourn is whether or not he inhaled. And to add grist to the mill, after Clinton left to become governor of Arkansas within 10 years, and later American president for eight years, a mid-1970s resident was Howard Marks, Britain's most prolific drug dealer!

Nor did it work out too well for Clinton. In 1998 he was impeached by the US House of Representatives on charges of perjury and obstruction of justice, although the Senate exonerated him. However, the charges meant that the Clinton name was besmirched and wife Hilary failed to make the White House. At least America eventually got Donald Trump.

Address 46 Leckford Road OX2 6HY | **Getting there** Bus 6 or 14 | **Hours** Viewable from the outside only | **Tip** Head the short trip east to newby St Antony's College, forever known as the spy's college thanks to John le Carré's *Tinker Tailor Soldier Spy* novel.

8 Binsey Poplars
Back by poplar demand!

These are no ordinary trees. The poplars of Binsey, one and a half miles north-west of the city centre, are only there thanks to the power of Gerard Manley Hopkins' poem entitled simply 'Binsey Poplars'. Although the work was published in 1918, 30 years after the great poet's death, the message was clear – 'how dare you chop them down. Replant the trees that line my walk along the Thames'!

Gerard Manley Hopkins (1844 – 89) was a Jesuit priest as well as a poet. His best-known line is 'Glory be to God for dappled things' from 'Pied Beauty', written in 1877, but also not published until 1918. Hopkins read Classics at Balliol and served as a parish priest at Oxford's St Aloysius Church. His description of Oxford is one of the greatest in poetry: 'Towery city and branchy between towers; Cuckoo-echoing, bell-swarmèd, lark charmèd, rook-racked, river-rounded'. The 'Binsey Poplars' poem captures his sadness and dismay at people's disregard for nature, which he saw as a symbol of God's power.

Hopkins believed everything in the universe had an individual design and purpose given to it by God. He led an austere and melancholic life, resulting in many poems of despair and desolation. Yet his dying words, at only 44, were: 'I am so happy, I am so happy. I loved my life'. Hopkins' success as a poet was posthumous, and he is credited with a unique use of rhythm and rhyme. 'Binsey Poplars' begins emphatically: 'My aspens dear, whose airy cages quelled / Quelled or quenched in leaves the leaping sun / All felled, felled, are all felle'. The poem becomes a metaphor for death; not a single tree 'that dandled a sandalled / Shadow that swam or sank / On meadow & river & wind-wandering weed-winding bank' was spared. To complete the sadness, the trees were chopped down again in 2004, but hope is eternal: Hopkins' poem helped raise funds for them to be replanted.

Address Thames Path, Binsey OX2 0NG | **Getting there** By car, take Binsey Lane from the A 420 and head north for about a mile, but the best way is on the Thames Path from near Oxford Station north | **Hours** Accessible 24 hours | **Tip** Head east to the Oxford Canal for Aristotle Bridge, so named on account of the philosophy lecturers who would stop here to ponder the meaning of life and what might be lurking in the dank depths below.

9 Blackbird Leys Banlieue

'White riot, I wanna riot…'

Mmm, Oxford is not all classy cloisters and ivy-covered colleges. In the south-east area of the city, conveniently just beyond the Eastern By-Pass, there is the notorious Blackbird Leys council estate that you don't see on the perfect picture postcards and that no one in the outside world knew existed until it all kicked off in 1991.

Blackbird Leys didn't have the best of starts in life. When planning permission was granted in 1953, the 260-acre site was occupied by a sewage works. The new estate would have 2,800 dwellings for 10,000 people.

Its purpose was to provide housing for the nearby Cowley car factory. In the unthinking mid-20th-century fashion, just one pub was opened, predictably called The Blackbird, and unfortunately selling the Ind Coope beer-like concoction.

Most of those jobs have gone, but the work left behind serious pollution and dereliction amidst the experimental utopian architecture and town planning that soon turned into a dystopian nightmare. The estate became known for a different sort of link with cars. In 1991, a spate of stealing high-powered motors and some serious joyriding on hot summer nights brought labels like 'Oxford's Toxteth' and led to Oxford's worst modern-day riots.

The outbreak that September followed a crackdown by police on joyriding. Some 150 youths stoned police officers and stopped an ambulance from reaching an injured woman as masked thugs hurled petrol bombs. To university historians, this was an unusual twist on the centuries-old town versus gown conflicts; this time, the workers had been moved out of the gown lands to the far edges of town and the opposition were workers in uniform. Oh the irony that politically motivated trouble could break out in the corner of a city with more Marxist and pseudo-Marxist intellectuals per head than anywhere else outside the Far East and bits of Belarus.

Address Blackbird Leys Road OX4 6HW | **Getting there** The estate is west off the B 480, south of its junction with the A 40 | **Hours** Accessible 24 hours | **Tip** Take a short drive, not in a hot rod, to marvel at the Cowley car works, home of the Mini.

10 Botanic Garden

Welcome to the garden of earthly delights

You've walked along High Street drunk with hedonistic indulgence at the wonders thereof. What more delights could there be? Well, there's this magnificent garden, the oldest of its kind in the country. The Botanic Garden occupies land that was partly a Jewish cemetery – until the Jews were expelled from England in 1290. It was founded by Henry Danvers as the Physic Garden in 1621 to grow plants for medicinal research, and was renamed the Botanic Garden in the 1830s. Entrance is on High Street, but not through the main arch, the Danby Gateway, as it is usually locked. Nevertheless, look up to see statues of Charles I (on the left) and Charles II (on the right). Above the kings is a statue of Danvers himself.

Once inside, take out your *Brideshead Revisited* and turn to this passage:

'Sebastian said: "Have some more Cointreau," so I stayed and later he said, "I must go to the Botanical Gardens."

"Why?"

"To see the ivy… there's a beautiful arch there and more different kinds of ivy than I knew existed. I don't know where I should be without the Botanical Gardens."'

The Botanic Garden also features in *Alice in Wonderland* (1865) in which Alice dreams of wandering 'among those beds of bright flowers'. In Philip Pullman's *His Dark Materials* series (1995–2000) Lyra and Will both promise to sit for an hour at noon on Midsummer's Day every year on a particular bench so that they might feel each other's presence.

After one particularly boisterous Bullingdon Club function, student Boris Johnson attempted to evade the police by crawling through a hedge in the Garden. He was caught, and spent the night in a police cell, which he claimed reduced him to 'a gibbering namby-pamby'. The rules here are excessive: no radios, ball games, dogs; no ice cream.

Address Rose Lane OX1 4AZ, +44 (0)1865 610300, www.obga.ox.ac.uk | Getting there
Bus 3, 3A, 8 or 10; the western end is a 12-minute walk from Oxford Station | Hours Daily
10am–4pm | Tip Head down adjacent Rose Lane to the River Cherwell with its gorgeous
views and vistas.

11 Brasenose Arms

Liege, Lief and Legend

There aren't many pubs in Britain where you can wander in and have a good chance of bumping into members of one of the most important groups of all time. For the Brasenose Arms and the village have long been associated with the remarkable Fairport Convention, doyens of the British folk rock scene, who were pictured outside the pub for the back cover of their 1973 album *Nine*. Every mid-August, Fairport and guest musicians assemble in a nearby Cropredy field for one of the most enjoyable and heart-warming music festivals of the year which, until Covid, was the country's longest running. The *bonhomie* they exude is infectious. This is musicianship of the highest calibre, wrought with a love of the traditional, the historic, of old rural England and simple pastoral pleasures.

Fairport Convention began in 1967, named after a house not in deepest rural Wessex, but a north London suburb. A founding member was Richard Thompson, guitarist and songwriter extraordinaire. Although they began with a distinct US West Coast feel, they quickly dropped the Jefferson Airplane postures to embrace the heart of Olde England, stunning the music world with songs as intense and disturbing as 'Who Knows Where the Time Goes?' and 'Fotheringay'. It is barely possible to believe that Thompson, scarcely out of his teens, could write a song as emotionally yearning as 'Farewell Farewell', which completed their greatest album, *Liege & Lief* from 1969.

But within a few years the band were beset by tragedy. An M1 crash killed drummer Martin Lamble. In 1971, a lorry smashed into the abandoned Hertfordshire pub where they were living and just missed killing half the band. In 1978, their best-known lead singer, the angelically voiced but traumatised Sandy Denny, died aged 31 when she fell downstairs. Yet Fairport continue as the longest regularly gigging band in modern music history.

Address Station Road, Cropredy OX17 1PW, +44 (0)1295 750244,
www.thebrasenose.co.uk | Getting there By car, leave the A 423 at Barnstones Caravan Park
and head north-east | Hours Daily noon – 10.30pm; tickets for the Fairport Convention
festival from www.fairportconvention.com | Tip There are some wonderful waterside walks
here, where the River Cherwell and the Oxford Canal run side by side.

12   Brasenose College
The brass nose of it!

What a magnificent and awe-inspiring sight is Thomas Graham Jackson's late 19th-century façade of Brasenose College on High Street. Brasenose, founded in 1509, is known as the 'happiest' college – successful sports teams, well-attended concerts and the ever-popular Arts Weeks. The college's strange name either comes from 'brasen huis' (brew house) or a brazen (brass or bronze) door knocker in the original building on the site, Brasenose Hall, which Oxford University bought in 1262. Noses have been used as symbols for Brasenose College for centuries, although students no longer get birched for conversing in English rather than Latin.

The college enjoys a fierce rivalry with Lincoln dating back to the 13th century when two Oxford students, one from Brasenose, one from Lincoln, were chased to the door of Lincoln College. The latter unhelpfully allowed only its own student entry, leaving the unfortunate Brasenoser to be beaten by townies. As a sign of remorse, each year on Ascension Day, Lincoln College students gain access to Brasenose through 'secret' tunnels and serve beer to their students.

Alumni include the heroic John Foxe (1516–87), author of the copious volume on the Catholic massacre of Protestants, *Foxe's Book of Martyrs* (1563). A hundred years later came Elias Ashmole (1617–92), astrologer, alchemist and royalist, who founded Oxford's Ashmolean Museum. According to one of the greatest of all Masonic conspiracy theories, it was Ashmole who gave up his life on 30 January, 1649 to be executed posing as Charles I as no executioner (all freemasons) would take the life of the leading mason in the land (the king).

More recently, Brasenose has given the world John Mortimer (1923–2009), the barrister who created Rumpole of the Bailey and successfully defended the Sex Pistols' right to call their groundbreaking 1977 punk album *Never Mind the Bollocks*.

Address Radcliffe Square OX1 4AJ | Getting there Bus 3, 3A, 8 or 10; the western end is a 12-minute walk from Oxford Station | Hours Guided tours Mon–Fri 10–11.30am & 2–4.30pm, Sat & Sun 1–4.30pm; individual tourists permitted at the discretion of the duty porter | Tip Opposite is The Ivy, not THE Ivy, but just the Oxford branch of what was originally *the* place for celebrities to be seen and occasionally eat in London.

13 Brasenose Lane

In the gutter, looking at the stars

Brasenose Lane is a must on the tasteful tourist trail. To the north are Exeter College and the Divinity School. To the south, Lincoln College, and beyond, Brasenose College, natch. At the eastern end stands the spectacular Radcliffe Camera.

A gutter in the middle of the street recalls less elegant times, however. Indeed, Brasenose Lane is the last in Oxford with a central channel or 'kennel' into which ran the filth of the district – rotting food, human refuse products, canine faeces and worse. Then there were the prostitutes, which was why the college windows were barred like those of a prison.

Fear stalked the air in 1827 following the murder of a young woman, Ann Crotchley, after drunken carousing with two students. A year later, the devil himself visited Brasenose Lane. Witnesses swore they saw a tall man in a long cloak outside the window of a student who was a member of the notorious Hell-Fire Club that shockingly promoted atheism. The student then unexpectedly died, the devil having arrived to claim his soul.

Even Oxford's greatest champion, 19th-century aesthete John Ruskin, who famously described the university as the 'Temple of Apollo', felt very differently about Brasenose Lane: 'In the centre of that temple, at the very foot of the dome of the Radclyffe, between two principal colleges, the lane by which I walked from my own college half an hour ago to this place – Brasen-nose Lane – is left in a state as loathsome as a back alley in the East End of London'.

Brasenose Lane's horrible history has drawn film makers and crime writers. Even James Bond in *Tomorrow Never Dies* from 1997. But it's not what it was. The toms have departed and the worst description anyone has managed to come up with in recent times referred to the 'almost perpetual stink of boiled cabbage from the Lincoln College kitchens'. Yes, what could be more horrible?

Address OX1 3DR | Getting there Bus 3, 3A, 6 or 8; the area is a 10- to 15-minute walk east from Oxford Station | Hours Accessible 24 hours | Tip Refreshment needed and so head to the ever-popular Turl Street Kitchen on nearby… Turl Street.

14 Brexit House
Taking back control

2016: the biggest democratic vote in British history. With the result through, the entire country united behind the push to leave the European Union, and the whole country has been as one since. Something like that. Nevertheless, as there were one or two detractors following the UK's vote to leave the European Union, the government has since hosted several secret summits involving cross-party politicians and Euro experts to sort out the mess – and the meetings have been taking place here at Ditchley Park.

The main topic has been 'how can we work better with our neighbours in Europe' amidst predictable calls of 'sell out' (Nigel Farage), a 'plot' (Lord David Frost) and 'a smug assemblage of arrogant establishment figures who think they know best' (*Daily Mail*). Leaks from journalists tell of secret cabals from within the already secret set-up to closely discuss such vital continental subjects as the exact length of the euro sausage and how Liverpool managed to get Barcelona to part with £142 million to buy Philippe Coutinho in January 2018.

Ditchley Park was built on a royal hunting ground in 1722 and designed by James Gibbs, who was also responsible for the glorious Radcliffe Camera in Oxford. In 1933, the property was bought by Tory MP Ronald Tree, one of the few who railed against the rise of Nazi Germany. As Chequers, Winston Churchill's official retreat as wartime PM, had an entrance road clearly visible from the sky in moonlight, he used Ditchley, masked by trees, as a country HQ. Indeed, Churchill asked Tree for 'accommodation at Ditchley for certain weekends, when the moon is high'. Here Churchill met presidential envoy Harry Hopkins as part of the campaign to win American support. The estate was later sold to David Wills of the tobacco family who set up the Ditchley Foundation to promote international relations and donated the house to a Trust.

Address Enstone, Chipping Norton OX7 4ER, +44 (0)1608 677346, www.ditchley.com |
Getting there The house is west of the A 44 at Over Kiddington. Charlbury Station is a mile
or so to the south-west. | Hours Join a government think-tank or become a Euro expert
MP to get an invitation. Alternatively, when Ditchley Park is not in use for conferences and
private events, guided tours are occasionally available, so check the website for details | Tip
Having solved the Brexit business, head a few miles east for some serious shopping therapy
at Bicester Village.

15 Bridge of Size

Looks more like the Rialto, mate

Although this much-loved 1914 Oxford landmark is known as the Bridge of Sighs, it looks more like Venice's Rialto. It's simply a means for students of Hertford College to access two parts of the college on either side of New College Lane. The bridge is just over 100 years old and was a regular in the *Inspector Morse* TV series. One ridiculous story connected to the bridge tells of a survey that found that Hertford students were the heaviest in Oxford. In response, Hertford barred them access to the bridge, forcing them to take the stairs instead.

Hertford College dates back to 1283, and was Alma Mater to one of the greatest writers in history, the 16th-century theologian William Tyndale, the first person to publish the Bible in English. Hertford was dissolved in 1805, but refounded in 1874. A hundred years later, in 1974, it was one of the first colleges to admit women. Famous alumni include Dom Mintoff, 1950s prime minister of Malta; Labour politician Jacqui Smith, home secretary (2007–09); and more importantly Evelyn Waugh, who wrote the greatest Oxford novel, *Brideshead Revisited* (1945). In the novel, the glamorous hero, Sebastian Flyte, returning from a Bullingdon Club bender, vomits through a window into the ground-floor room of a building on the northern side of the college quad.

Waugh was full of witty aphorisms: 'You spend your first term at Oxford meeting interesting and exciting people and the rest of your time avoiding them.' In Waugh's time, the dean and principal was Charles Cruttwell. Waugh and his pals were convinced Cruttwell was sexually attracted to dogs and used to stand outside his window at night barking. More worryingly, a later college principal was Will Hutton, former editor of the once-great now-declining *Observer* Sunday newspaper, and author of the somehow best-seller *The State We're In* (1995). He's gone now.

Address Holywell Street at Catte Street OX1 3BW | Getting there Bus 3, 3A, 8 or 10; a 20-minute walk from Oxford Station | Hours Viewable from the outside only | Tip Book tickets for a concert at the Holywell Music Room on Holywell Street. Not only the city's venue for chamber concerts, but the oldest purpose-built music room in Europe.

16 __ Britain's Oldest Chemist
I'm not putting that down my shirt!

Just think how wonderful medicine was in 1734 when Reavley's chemist's predecessor opened. Popular drugs of the day included mercury and arsenic, serious poison to most knowledgeable people. And if that wasn't bad enough, hemlock and deadly nightshade were always available. Bleeding was popular, based on the ancient belief that blood contained the illness. Remove the blood, remove the illness. Doctors would open a vein and remove a pint, nearly an armful as a Georgian Tony Hancock probably put it. And if you had some serious ackers, you could always obtain gold-coated opium pills. Why didn't someone just invent penicillin?

This building dates back to 1401, as far as the original timbers are concerned, and was originally a coaching inn, *Novum Hospitium Angulare* – New Pub on the Corner, in English. Eyres, the Royalist general, used it as his HQ during the English Civil War, Nicholas Willet turned it into a chemist in 1734, and in Victorian times the shop was furnished with traditional mahogany, apothecary drawers and cabinets, each with a painted label denoting the contents, which remain in place.

Customers now come for 100-year-old traditional remedies such as Zam-Buk, which heals cuts and relieves dry or sore skin. Basilicon ointment draws out splinters. Bengue's Balsam contains such wonderful products as menthol, wintergreen and beeswax; add a little boiling water for a steamy recipe to relieve a blocked nose. Zinc Ointment comes with a warning not to use it as sun screen protection. Nooo. The weirdest is Lion Ointment, made not from the bones of the gigantic raging cat but from a time-honoured formula as an antiseptic for minor skin conditions. What no one suffers from any more is the 1950s Iris Murdoch-ish ailment of chilblains. But if you have come out of a time warp with the affliction, then Robert Reavley's 1930 remedy will ease the burning sensation.

Address Reavley Chemist, 124 High Street, Burford OX18 4QR, +44 (0)1993 823144, www.reavley.co.uk | Getting there Burford is right on the A40 with the High Street to the north | Hours Mon–Fri 9am–6pm, Sat 9am–5pm | Tip In the heart of Burford, near St John the Baptist Hall, is Warwick Hall, which was transformed into a derelict village hall for the TV version of J. K. Rowling's *A Casual Vacancy*.

17 _ Carfax Tower
Four ways to go

The very centre of Oxford and, some say, the very centre of the Earth, is Carfax. The name comes from *Quadrifurcus* – four forks – because here four roads from the four old city gates meet, the four roads being St Aldate's, Cornmarket, Queen Street and High Street.

The junction is dominated by the 13th-century tower of what was St Martin's Church. If the tower looks a little forlorn, that's because the rest of the church was pulled down in 1896. Medieval St Martin's was the official civic church for the city, where one William Shakespeare acted as godfather to the future poet laureate, William Davenant. The first church was demolished in 1820, leaving just this tower. The second church opened in 1822, but lasted only 70 years. All Saints on High Street then became the civic church until that was converted into Lincoln College's library in 1976.

The excuse for pulling down the second St Martin's was to improve traffic flow. Unfortunately, the council has now turned that on its head, needlessly pedestrianising Queen Street, the road that leads west, creating unnecessary traffic jams and making part of the city centre look like Wigan, but not even doing it properly, as pedestrians discover when a hybrid bus glides silently towards their unsuspecting behind.

The clock on the east side of Carfax Tower is a copy of the original. It sports mechanical figures, quarter boys, that hammer out the quarter-hour on a pair of Victorian bells and are rung on special occasions, such as an alumnus being made prime minister. A stone in the north side of the tower reads: 'Peace was proclaimed in the city of Oxford', referring to the year Napoleon was imprisoned on Elba, but the date that should be with it, 27 June, 1814, has worn away.

Climb to the top of the 74-foot high tower for excellent views, and marvel how a local by-law asserts that no Oxford building can be higher than Carfax Tower.

Address Queen Street OX1 1ET | **Getting there** Oxford Station – most Oxford buses
go through the junction | **Hours** Mostly 10am–3pm, later during summer months | **Tip**
A plaque on the Santander bank at the south-west corner of Carfax recalls the Swindlestock
Tavern where, in 1355, a fight between two students and a tavern keeper over the quality of
the beer led to two days of violence known as the St Scholastica Day Riots. For centuries
the mayor and councillors had to walk, their heads uncovered, through the streets on St
Scholastica's Day to pay a penny fine for each student killed (a total of 5s 3d).

18 Cash Controversy College

No pasarán!

St Peter's is a college you don't mess with. Founded in 1929 by Francis Chavasse, Bishop of Liverpool, its most famous alumnus is Ken Loach, the one-time fiercely watchable film director now turned arch foaming-at-the-mouth anti-Zionist. But if that isn't bad enough, in 2021, the college accepted a £5 million pound donation from a trust set up by the late Max Mosley, hardcore fascist, and one of the most insidious and iniquitous characters of recent British politics.

The Mosley family notoriety remains. Oswald Mosley, Max Mosley's father, was a Tory MP, switched to Labour, became a minister, but is best known as the 1930s leader of the violent, psychopathic, racist, anti-Semitic British Union of Fascists. His mother was Diana Mitford, who married Mosley in the home of the Nazi propaganda minister, Joseph Goebbels, with Hitler as guest of honour. Max Mosley long supported his father's politics and took part in fascist attacks in his youth. He graduated from Christ Church, Oxford, in physics, became a barrister, but conveniently began to conceal his views as he forged a career in British motor racing.

Technically, the donations were in the name of the Alexander Mosley Charitable Trust, named after Mosley's son, an Oxford graduate, brilliant mathematical economist, but a long-term heroin addict, who died at the age of 39. His cousin, Olivia Channon, died of a heroin overdose in 1986 in the Christ Church College Oxford rooms of Count Gottfried von Bismarck, playboy descendant of Germany's greatest statesman, who himself later died of a heroin overdose.

The donations horrified morally upstanding members of Oxford University. Professor Lawrence Goldman, emeritus Fellow in History at St Peter's, told journalists that the donations 'are tainted with dirty money and should be going to the communities who were terrorised and beaten up by [Oswald] Mosley and his thugs'. St Peter's has now expressed its disgust at 'discrimination'. Wow.

Address New Inn Hall Street OX1 2DL, +44 (0)1865 278900, www.spc.ox.ac.uk | Getting there Bus 6 or 13; Oxford Station is nearby | Hours Open for visitors 10am–5pm | Tip Seek forgiveness nearby in St Ebbe's Church, part of the Anglican Reform movement.

19 Caudwell's Castle

Bringing home the bacon

It's not really a castle, although it looks like one, and it's now just apartments. But it's still called Caudwell's Castle because it's the work of Joseph Caudwell, a Victorian eccentric who built this monstrosity on Folly Bridge Island on the Thames, amusing locals with its white plaster sculptures, statues of chess bishops, oddly dotted wrought-iron balconies, crenellations, brass cannons and, on the roof, Atlas who has lost his globe.

Pevsner described Caudwell's Castle as a 'bit of a joke'. But it was no joke when, in 1851, a student tried to drag one of the cannons into the river. Caudwell shot and seriously wounded the bounder, but was found not guilty on the grounds that the student had behaved deplorably. Indeed, the judge noted how the accused 'after luxuriating at a cricket club supper at Maidenhead, smoking cigars and drinking beer, sallied forth, and in order to fill up or rather to kill time, proceeded to this man's house for wanton mischief, and to despoil his premises, for the sake of gratifying a morbid and wicked disposition'. In an unrelated incident, Caudwell was later found guilty of perjury, fined a shilling, and transported for seven years.

Caudwell built this folly in homage of the demolished brick fortress that stood here for centuries and had been home to Friar Roger Bacon, the influential 13th-century philosopher and astronomer. Samuel Pepys was a visitor on Tuesday 9 June, 1668: 'So to Friar Bacon's study: I up and saw it, and give the man a bottle of Sack for the landlord.' In the 20th century, Caudwell's Castle became a brothel. By 1980, it was in a poor state of repair and was sold for only £48,000.

This has always been a lively location, with boatyards, locks, basins and now the popular Head of the River pub. Alongside was an ancient ford where oxen crossed the river – the derivation of the name Oxford.

Address 5 Folly Bridge OX1 4LB | Getting there Bus 1, 5 or 5A; Oxford Station is 10 minutes to the west | Hours Viewable from the outside only | Tip Right here is a rare late Georgian toll house, built in the 1840s to nab those coming from the Grandpont area in search of the new railway station.

20 __ Cherwell Magazine HQ

A river runs through it

Oxford's student newspaper, laced with more sarcasm and sniping even than *Private Eye*, written in a tone of relentless irony, so detractors say, is named after Oxford's other river. Its contributors include some of the greatest writers of the last 100 years – John Betjeman, Evelyn Waugh, Graham Greene, as well as Jeffrey Archer.

Cherwell was founded in 1920 by two Balliol students, Cecil Binney and George Edinger, who later recalled its radical voice: 'We were feeling for a new Oxford....We were anti-convention, anti-Pre War values, pro-feminist.' But not that progressive. It was the only newspaper printed in Britain during the 1926 General Strike, and in 1946 the university banned the paper for distributing a survey on the sex lives of undergraduates. Not to be outdone, eight years later, they produced pin-up photos of 'Girls of the Year'.

Cherwell was short of money in the 1950s. Then help came from the Union treasurer, the future Tarzan, Michael Heseltine, and it became a newspaper. This led to a bit of a barney with Oxford's rivals, Cambridge, who wanted to publish an Oxford version of their paper, *Varsity*. A dozen Cambridge *Varsity* contributors hit Oxford on 24 January, 1955 to flypost, but their bumf was torn down by Cherwellians. The BBC even sent journalists hoping to film 'a bit of scuffling' between the two. Michael Winner, the eventual pulp film director, was then editor of *Varsity*. He kept a low profile in Oxford as he had heard that the *Cherwell* staff wanted to throw him into the river.

Funds remained short, but celebs approached for money were reticent. In 1974 the comic writer Kingsley Amis, ex-Oxford, responded: 'I understand your difficulty, but I am rather hard up these days, and since *Cherwell* never did anything for me in the way of publishing my work, I don't see why I should go out of my way to do something for it.' Quite.

Address 7 St Aldate's OX1 1BS, +44 (0)1865 722780, www.cherwell.org | Getting there Bus 1, 5 or 5A; Oxford Station is 10 minutes to the west | Hours By appointment, but you can read *Cherwell* online any time | Tip For a more pastoral experience, head west to St Ebbe's Church, redesigned in 2017 by Quinlan Terry, King Charles' favourite architect.

21 __ Christ Church Meadow

A road doesn't run through it

It's about as close as you can get to paradise on Earth this side of the old walled city of Jerusalem and the Hanging Gardens of Babylon. Christ Church Meadow is the one location that every visitor to Oxford gravitates towards, and which attracts every local every day, because they can't believe it exists.

The meadow is the perfect example of *rus in urbe*, the countryside in the city idyll first described by Martial, the Latin epigrammatist, who never went to Oxford, some time around the year A.D. 60. Stroll through the avenue of lime and poplar trees; idle along the glorious riverside walks where you might spot the crews training for the Boat Race (in which Oxford always manages to come first or second); and head to the fence for the chance of meeting some masticating longhorn cattle, an historic breed of cow that was the first dedicated to the production of beef in England. The meadow is even the setting for the start of the boat trips that Charles Dodgson (Lewis Carroll) took with the friends who inspired the characters in *Alice in Wonderland*.

If that's not enough, there's the chance of being speechless in admiration at the view of the divine Christ Church Meadow building, Thomas Deane of Dublin's Venetian Gothic wonder of the 1860s, which provides one of the most famous and best-loved sights in the city. And yet not everyone has been grateful. Lewis Perry Curtis, a 1950s American student who became a leading historian, derided the Christ Church Meadow building as 'a huge and ungainly pile of Ruskinian Gothic'. It got even worse the next decade. Nihilist antisocial council officials announced that they would build a relief road right through the meadow. This totally pointless destructive measure shocked all right-thinking people. Thank God it was scrapped, and the result was the formation of the Oxford Civic Society to protect the city's heritage.

Address South of Broad Walk OX1 4JF | **Getting there** Bus 1, 5 or 5A; Oxford Station is 10 minutes to the west | **Hours** Accessible 24 hours | **Tip** Spend hours strolling along the many river walks in this watery part of Oxford.

22 — City Wall
And the walls came tumbling down – most of them

They're in a better state than the walls of Jericho – Jericho, Israel, not Jericho, Oxford, that is. The ancient walls of Oxford can be seen across the city. Some sections survive in surprising locations. Sometimes the wall goes inside a college or across its garden, barely accessible to the public. The walls were built because Oxford had to be defended; it stands at a strategic position by the River Thames, at its junction with the River Cherwell. Saxons, Vikings, Normans, out-of-town oiks, students from Cambridge and various ne'er-do-wells had to be repelled. The wall was built on the Mercian side of the river. On the other side was Berkshire, which was in a different kingdom: Wessex.

The earliest walls were made of turf with a timber palisade, later replaced by stone. There were gates so that folk could get in and out. Amazingly, the North Gate still has its Saxon tower, now part of the church of St Michael on Cornmarket Street. The South Gate spanned the street that is now St Aldate's, which, interestingly, used to be known as Great Jewry Street. Nevertheless, its church, St Michael-at-the-Southgate, was demolished by Thomas Wolsey in the 1520s to make way for Christ Church. The East Gate was on High Street, just east of Merton Street, and included St Peter-in-the-East Church, which survives. The West Gate stood at the junction of the present-day Castle and Paradise streets, hence the Westgate shopping centre.

The walls fell into disrepair in late medieval times and the moat became a fishpond. The Mileways Act of road improvements in 1771 saw the removal of the surviving town gates, but here, on the north side of Brewer Street, the wall survives, supporting Pembroke College. So too does the well-known Oxford rhyme:

'At North-Gate and at South-Gate too / St Michael guards the way,
While o'er the East and o'er the West / St Peter holds his sway.'

Address Brewer Street OX1 1QN | **Getting there** Bus 1, 5 or 5A; Oxford Station is 10 minutes to the west | **Hours** Accessible 24 hours; a leaflet and map of the walls is available from the Tourist Information Centre at 15–16 Broad Street OX1 3AS, +44 (0)1865 252200. Alternatively, download a self-guided walk from www.oxfordpreservation.org.uk | **Tip** No defence needed for visiting St Philip's bookshop at 82 St Aldate's, specialists in rare and second-hand books.

23 — Classy Keble
Polychromatic pièce-de-résistance

Kenneth Clark, the famed art historian, described it as the 'ugliest building in the world'. The reality is that Keble is one of the wonders of Oxford. The architect was William Butterfield, one of the greatest Gothic revivalists of the 19th century. Swoon at the differently coloured bricks and stonework, marvel at the crockets and tiny spires, suspire at the religious symbolism. Butterfield went to extraordinary lengths. He designed the college's Liddon Quad by heaving huge amounts of earth onto the sunken ground. Yet none of this impressed Clark, nor the probably apocryphal Frenchman who walked by one day and marvelled at how beautiful the railway station was.

John Keble founded the college in 1870 for 'gentlemen wishing to live economically'. Originally it taught mostly theology, but later broadened to science – same sort of thing really. Try to visit to view the dining hall, the biggest in Oxford, which can feed 300 people on long wooden benches surrounded by portraits of past college greats. Talking of which, they include legendary cricketer and not so legendary Pakistan premier Imran Khan; TV writer Frank Cottrell Boyce; and Lord Adonis, the Labour politician who cleverly devised HS2 on the back of an envelope thereby making Britain's rail plans a laughing stock.

Keble's prize possession is a copy of Pre-Raphaelite artist William Holman Hunt's *The Light of the World* (1851–54), which Van Gogh described as the 'supreme depiction of Christ'. But is it the right one? There are three *Light of the World*s, with one in the crypt of St Paul's Cathedral and another in Manchester Art Gallery. Experts are not sure which one is by his pupil, Fred Stephens. But trouble is brewing. Researchers have discovered to their horror that late 19th-century PM William Gladstone once gave the college £200, and Gladstone père was a slave trader. Unbelievable. Close the place down!

Address Keble Road OX1 3PG, +44 (0)1865 272727, www.keble.ox.ac.uk | Getting there Bus 2 or 14; a 20-minute walk from Oxford Station | Hours Daily 2–5pm | Tip Wait for summer and the chance of seeing some proper sleepy cricket at the nearby Parks ground.

24 Covered Market

Oxford's market forces

A must is to shop here in what is one of the classier indoor markets in the country. Quality goods, pleasant atmosphere; a few thousand steps up from similar markets in Huddersfield or Stretford. The Covered Market opened on 1 November, 1774 and meant that the streets would no longer be filled with rotting carcasses and awful offal. It became the only place where meat, poultry and fish could be sold legally. Fish Street became St Aldates and Butcher Row Queen Street. The market has been regularly rebuilt and extended over the centuries. Its first architect, John Gwynn, who also designed Magdalen Bridge, would recognise only the three-arched stone façade on High Street.

The market is filled with small family-run businesses, and gives locals and visitors an experience that sees them leave the premises with a smile on their face and a bargain in the bag, compared with the depressing maelstrom that emanates from a visit to the Westgate shopping centre.

Who knows what you might spot? A haunch of venison, a row of pheasants, dangling rabbits, the flowers that are obligatory for exams. Who knows who you might spot? Wills and Kate have been here, tucking into specialist cheeses and sipping Colombian coffee, hand-crafted and artisan, whatever those are. The most popular produce is the Oxford sausage. Never mind the secrecy that infamously envelopes the make-up of Coca Cola; it's the ingredients of the Oxford sausage that are seriously hush-hush. However, we can reveal that pork and veal play a part along with a secret blend of spices, lemon, herbs and sausagey bits.

You never know what sort of bizarre event might take place here. Richard Hawkins, a boatman on the Oxford Canal, astounded shoppers one day in 1789 when he offered his wife for sale by auction in the market. William Gibbs, a stonemason working on the nearby canal, bought her for five shillings.

Address There are four entrances on High Street and four on Market Street. Try the one between Nos. 16 and 17 High Street OX1 4AG, www.oxford-coveredmarket.co.uk | **Getting there** Bus 3, 3A, 8 or 10; the western end is a 12-minute walk from Oxford Station | **Hours** Mon – Sat 8am – 5.30pm, Sat & Sun 10am – 4pm but individual traders may keep different hours | **Tip** Hungry for more market shopping? Head west to the Gloucester Green Outdoor Market, where you can find everything from fruit and veg to plants, pet food and haberdashery.

25 Crocodiles of the World
See you later, alligator

They're the most dangerous beasts on the planet. They'll bite the arm or leg off the unwary swimmer and that's just a snack before lunch. But what the hell are they doing in Oxfordshire? Surely they belong in Florida or Mozambique?

The Crocodiles of the World zoo opened in 2011 so that intrepid members of the public could come face to face with some of the world's most feared predators in what they describe as a 'fun' environment. Yes, if you stay out of the water. Hold on; these beasts can ravage on dry land as well. The venue offers underwater viewing and thankfully encounters with rather more hospitable animals such as otters, Galapagos tortoises, a Komodo dragon (the world's largest lizard) and meerkats, fresh from the *Coronation Street* ads, no doubt. There are even special spots at feeding time. Just don't whistle Jimmy Nail's 'Alligator Shoes'.

As far as the main attractions are concerned, you can see endangered Siamese crocodiles, Chinese alligators, Nile crocodiles and American alligators. The Saltwater crocodile, nearly 20 feet long, is the largest of all living reptiles and the biggest terrestrial predator in the world. No, it won't get out. According to the experts, the rarest of the beasts is the endangered Philippine crocodile which, can you believe, 'has an image problem with outsiders'. You don't say! The good news is that it will only attack – and eat – people if provoked. Crocodiles of the World also offers an adult croc experience to meet the residents and provide them with the fish of the day. Rather more leisured is the chance to meet the 100-year-old Galapagos tortoises: Dirk, the largest in Britain, along with his female companions Zuzu, Isabella and Charlie.

Visitors often ask: 'What's the difference between an alligator and a crocodile?' The answer is easy. An alligator will eat you up without a second's thought. And so will a crocodile.

Address Burford Road, Brize Norton, Carterton OX18 3NX, +44 (0)1993 846353, www.crocodilesoftheworld.co.uk | Getting there By car, take the B 4477 just north of Brize Norton and look out for chomping jaws or more sedate signs | Hours Daily 10am–5pm (last admission 4pm) – visitor numbers are limited, so it is best to book | Tip Explore nearby Kilkenny Lane Country Park, where the most dangerous animal you're likely to encounter is a hungry pigeon.

26 Deadman's Walk

Bring out the bodies

The few locals or visitors who are ever seen taking this path, which runs east–west between Merton College and Christ Church Meadow, are those who don't know its name or the stories surrounding it. For, according to legend, this was the route taken by medieval Jewish coffin-carrying processions. The funeral party would begin their slow mournful march at the synagogue that stood near where Tom Tower now stands on St Aldate's, in those days Great Jewry Street. They would then head for the Jewish burial ground that is now the Botanic Garden (see ch. 10). Just to make matters really annoying, the party would have to cross two wide water courses running up to arches at the foot of Merton College wall, one of which was big enough for a rowing boat.

When the would-be queen, Matilda, took root in Oxford Castle in the 1130s, she demanded money from the Jews of Oxford. After her surprise escape from Oxford Castle, the alternative monarch, Stephen, also demanded money from the already taxed Jewish community. When they objected, Stephen burned down the house of a local Jew, Aaron, and threatened the same on the rest of the community unless they paid up. Jews were banned from burying their dead within the city walls, so they bought a water meadow for a burial ground, now occupied by Magdalen College, outside the walls. In 1231, the Hospital of St John the Baptist took over the land, and a small section was given to the Jews for a new cemetery. But in 1290 Edward I expelled all Jews from England. They were not permitted to return for more than 350 years.

A less romantic story has it that the name Deadman's Walk comes from an ancient field with a tumulus or burial mound. But there is another reason why. It might be haunted by the ghost of Francis Windebank, a Royalist colonel and spy executed by firing squad in 1645 against the wall here that borders Merton College.

Address Deadman's Walk OX1 4JD | **Getting there** Bus 3, 3A, 8 or 10; a 12-minute walk from Oxford Station | **Hours** Accessible 24 hours | **Tip** While you're here, book a visit to nearby Merton College (www.merton.ox.ac.uk).

27 — The Devil's Quoits
Satan's been and gone, and left us his stones

Surprised at the name? Don't be. The name Devil's Quoits comes from a legend that the Devil once played quoits with a beggar, hoping to gain his soul, while sitting on the top of Wytham Hill, which provides a commanding view across the Thames Valley, and won by flinging these great stones around.

Here in Wessex there is a series of prehistoric monuments, ring ditches and mortuaries. This henge is Neolithic, between 4,000 and 5,000 years old, and is a Scheduled Ancient Monument. Within the henge, there used to be a stone circle that originally featured 36 stones. Much of the circle was destroyed by farmers in the Middle Ages, and by the 20th century only three stones were still standing, and the earthworks could barely be seen. When it came to World War II, the authorities announced that the whole site was to be levelled for a runway, which meant a field of concrete – not an ancient henge's best friend. But come on, a war was on. The base was used for the raid on the German battleship Scharnhorst and was where Winston Churchill left for the vital 1943 Casablanca Conference.

Soon there was only one stone still standing in the right place. The site was then further damaged by gravel extraction. But ancient sites have more power than airfields. By 1985, the runway had been removed. Even better, new archaeological excavations between 2002 and 2008 saw many original stones discovered, having been buried in the ditch, and the Quoits were restored to what experts believed were their condition in Roman times when ploughing began, while the surrounding earthworks was rebuilt. It is hard to believe this is mostly a reconstruction and not an undiscovered Stonehenge. Local druids and paganists are happy, even if some of the disused air strip buildings are still in place rotting away. In a thousand years' time they too will have assumed ancient historic status.

Address Main Road, Stanton Harcourt, Witney OX29 5BB | **Getting there** Head to Stanton Harcourt Cricket Club, and then west towards the lake | **Hours** Accessible 24 hours | **Tip** Head north to the lovely market town of Witney by the River Windrush, famous for its blanket making and traditional buildings.

28 Dictionary Editor's Post
He gives you his word

How clever of the Post Office to place a post box next to a plaque for Sir James Murray (1837–1915), originator of the Oxford English Dictionary. While living here, Murray not only received many tons of mail helping him with his compiling, but also had to send out innumerable letters through this very box seeking clarification of meanings.

Murray started work on the epic tome in the 1870s. In a fit of Johnsonian (Dr, not Boris) pique, he vowed to complete the dictionary in 10 years, but by the time he died in 1915 he had finished less than half. Murray adopted many of Johnson's (Dr, not Boris) explanations without change, although not *oats* – 'a grain, which in England is generally given to horses, but in Scotland supports the people'. Working with him in 1920, was J. R. R. Tolkien who parodied Murray and his fellow editors as 'The Four Wise Clerks of Oxenford' in his story 'Farmer Giles of Ham'. The most remarkable contributor was a Dr William Chester Minor who would send in some 20 quotations a day. Murray wanted to meet him and was staggered to discover the doctor was a patient at Broadmoor Asylum. He was a murderer!

The dictionary was first published in 1929 and has to be constantly updated because annoying people keep on inventing new words – binge-watch, bling, box-set, Brexit – and those are just the Bs. No wonder they're up to half a million entries. The most pretentious word is still antidisestablishmentarianism, a religious term, recently and predictably used by Jacob Rees-Mogg in the House. But it's not just definitions; there are literary allusions to be considered. In the old days, there would be hundreds of slips with such references; now it's all stored on the computer (Dictionary deffo: one who computes; a calculator, reckoner).

The post box here strangely doesn't contain any royal insignia (e.g. Victoria Regina) or even the words 'Post Office'.

Monday to Friday
9.00am
Saturday
7.00am

Address Sunnyside, 78 Banbury Road OX2 6JT | **Getting there** Bus 2, 2A or 14; a 30-minute walk from Oxford Station | **Hours** Accessible 24 hours | **Tip** Around the corner on Linton Road is the Pasternak Trust featuring the work of Leonid, leading Russian artist, and his better-known son Boris, author of *Dr Zhivago* (1957).

29 Door of Bocardo Prison
Lock up yer martyrs

Just the door survives of the jail that held the Protestant leaders, Hugh Latimer, Nicholas Ridley and Thomas Cranmer, who were executed nearby (see ch. 64) in the 1550s. It's located here in the Saxon bell tower of St Michael at the North Gate church, the oldest structure in the city.

St Michael's dates back to 1020 and is built in coral ragstone. It was part of the city's medieval defences, opening on the north gate. There the town stationed military hardware ready to 'cast downe anything obnoxious to the enemy approaching thereunto', according to Anthony Wood, the 17th-century historian. The name Bocardo came from the word 'boggard', a privy, denoting the insanitary nature of the premises.

Its most remarkable prisoner was John of Powderham, who challenged Edward II's right to the throne early in the 14th century. Powderham was an Oxford clerk who took advantage of Edward's unpopularity and arrived at the city's Beaumont Palace, claiming to be Edward himself thanks to some similarity in appearance, even though he was missing a crucial ear. He was hanged in 1318.

Elizabeth Fletcher, one of the first Quakers, was imprisoned here in the 1650s. Her party piece was to walk naked through the streets of Oxford to show how false teachings could be stripped away. Surprisingly, she was roughly treated, chased by college students who flogged and beat Fletcher, pumped water over her and whipped her out of the city, causing her to sustain an injury that hastened her death at the age of 19.

The Bocardo later added a separate wing for prostitutes as well as a debtors' prison, or Bridewell, from which inmates would hang a bag hoping for donations from generous passers-by. The prison was demolished in 1771. During Covid in 2020 the church bore a welcoming sign saying: 'We were here during the Black Death in 1347 and we were here during the Great Plague in 1665'.

Address Cornmarket Street OX1 3EY | Getting there Bus 6 or 13; Oxford Station is nearby | Hours The church is open daily 9am – 5pm | Tip Cornmarket, the very busy street outside, is no ordinary high street. Sadly, much of it has been spoiled by unsightly shop fronts, but move your gaze to the upper floors and you'll see a fascinating mix of architectural styles remaining.

30 Dreaming Spires
Climb St Mary's tower for a spectacular view

It's one of the most over-used clichés in British tourism: Oxford, 'city of dreaming spires'. But that's because the city really is filled with the most glorious buildings, created in the Romanesque and Gothic styles, with a consistency of colour and tone that visitors and locals can never believe exists.

Much of Oxford is late medieval, laid out in a geometric and accessible style, hewn from gorgeous buff Cotswold stone. Here you won't find the eyesores that disfigure Manchester and Birmingham. Instead, picturesque college after picturesque college, many of which can be savoured from the top of St Mary's, which gives one of the best views in the city.

Typical is New College, considered one of the most significant medieval buildings of its kind in Europe, and an excellent example of English Perpendicular Gothic. It was one of the first colleges to lay out its main buildings of chapel, hall, library and dorms around a quadrangle in a format that became the model for later colleges. Better still, the college and gardens are enclosed by 13th-century town walls.

The phrase 'dreaming spires' comes from Victorian poet Matthew Arnold and his 1865 poem *Thyrsis* with the line 'that sweet city with her dreaming spires'. Arnold wrote *Thyrsis* in honour of his friend, the poet Arthur Hugh Clough, who died in November 1861 aged only 42. Arnold's view of Oxford was from Boars Hill, three miles south-west of the city centre, a suburb that became a favourite address for a number of 20th-century poets including Robert Bridges, John Masefield and Robert Graves. But it was in his 'Essays in Criticism' that Arnold conceived the city's finest tribute: 'Beautiful city! so venerable, so lovely, so unravaged by the fierce intellectual life of our century, so serene!… spreading her gardens to the moonlight, and whispering from her towers the last enchantments of the Middle Age.'

Address High Street OX1 4BJ, +44 (0)1865 279111, www.universitychurch.ox.ac.uk | Getting there Bus 3, 3A, 8 or 10; the western end is a 12-minute walk from Oxford Station | Hours Mon – Sat 9.30am – 5pm, Sun noon – 5pm, although the tower may be closed at short notice in bad weather | Tip After all that climbing, relax opposite at the Jericho Coffee Traders, named not after Jericho, Israel, but Jericho, Oxford (www.jerichocoffeetraders.com).

31 Dusty Springfield's Grave
Not in the middle of nowhere

No one in Memphis in 1968 could believe that the husky-voiced singer cutting an album with the greatest soul musicians of the day at the city's American Sound Studio came from Hampstead, London, not Holly Springs, Mississippi. But Mary Isabel Catherine Bernadette O'Brien became one of Britain's greatest singers as Dusty Springfield after launching her career alongside her brother Tom O'Brien in the early 1960s.

After a string of banal pop hits, she achieved legendary status with her cover of Burt Bacharach's 'I Just Don't Know What To Do With Myself'. Dusty's image of peroxide bouffant and thick black eyeliner propelled her into the nation's consciousness. To prove her soul credentials, she joined Atlantic Records in New York. They sent her to the Deep South to work with the leading producers of the day, Tom Dowd (*Layla*) and Jerry Wexler (Aretha Franklin's hits), to create the groundbreaking album, *Dusty in Memphis*, which the US Library of Congress has added to the National Recording Registry of recordings deemed culturally, historically or aesthetically significant.

Dusty's career stalled in the 1970s, but a surprise revival came in 1987 thanks to the Pet Shop Boys and the chart success 'What Have I Done to Deserve This?', soon followed with what became her greatest achievement, 'Nothing Has Been Proved', from the film *Scandal* about the corrupt Tory MP John Profumo. Dusty Springfield moved to Henley and lived in a five-bedroom riverfront house, but died of breast cancer in 1999. Her gravestone is here at St Mary's and her ashes were scattered at the cliffs of Moher in Ireland. Each year fans gather in the town to celebrate Dusty Day on the closest Sunday to her 16 April birthday. Recently, the mayor has discussed reviving the celebration that used to take place at the Slug and Lettuce pub, now Coppa Club, as part of Henley's gay pride celebrations.

Address St Mary's Church, Hart Street, Henley RG9 2AT | Getting there Hart Street is the A 4130; Henley Station is a short distance south | Hours Churchyard accessible 24 hours, but best not visit the grave in the dark! | Tip Head to Stonor Park, four miles north of Henley, for the mansion and Tumblestone Hollow adventure playground for kids of all ages.

32 The Embarrassed College
Worcester's cross to bear

Oxford colleges win all sorts of awards, but Worcester has topped the lot when it comes to triumphing in the unwanted snowflakery Cowardly Cancellers of the Year stakes. In 2021 they apologised for holding a Christian youth camp after students complained they were 'distressed' by attendees approaching them and aggressively, wait for it, handing out leaflets bearing Christian ideas.

One might have thought delegates had swarmed along Beaumont Street brandishing flaming crosses. Worcester College was reminded that there has been at least a smidgeon of sympathy for Christian beliefs in Britain since Joseph of Arimathea arrived fresh from the Crucifixion to let the traders of Cornwall know that the young Jesus wouldn't be wanting a fresh stash of tin, round about the year A.D. 30.

The college claimed that the views expressed at the conference did not 'align' with their 'values'. David Isaac, then Provost of Worcester and the former head of the Equality and Human Rights Commission, told students that 'our normal vetting processes did not work', and that letting Christian Concern use the college facilities was 'a serious failure'. Naturally, the freedom of speech movement had a monty, and Isaac was reminded that the whole point of Oxford University and its 44 colleges was to discuss challenging ideas without fear of censorship. Worcester was accused of unlawfully discriminating against Christians – 'wrapping up its bigotry as support for diversity', as the *Telegraph* put it.

Interestingly, the institution has recently been known as 'the People's Republic of Worcester College', thanks to former Interim Provost Dr Kate Tunstall who wanted to abolish much-loved college traditions such as saying grace before meals. Typically, her social media profile showed support for the most pressing political Oxford issue of all – Palestine. Worcester is still open for new students.

Address Worcester Street OX1 2HB, +44 (0)1865 278300, www.worc.ox.ac.uk | Getting there Bus 6 or 13; Oxford Station is nearby | Hours Daily 2–4pm for local residents, pre-booked via the Porters' Lodge; may be open to the general public so call the Porters' Lodge for up-to-date information | Tip Free yourself of the stress of fashionable political pomposity by heading west to explore the picturesque Oxford Canal.

33 — English Government, 1640s
Royalist government on the run

Nowadays to see Parliament in action, you join a queue at Westminster, spend half an hour going through security, and when you get inside there are three sleeping MPs and the member for Toryshire South talking to himself about the Water Voles Act (1973).

In 1640s Oxford it was so much easier. The king had moved the capital here, and his government was everywhere – Christ Church, Bodleian Library, The House of Lords in the Geometry school and here, Convocation House, now part of the Divinity School, just north of Brasenose Lane, being where his parliament met. When the Royal Mint arrived as well, all colleges were asked to donate their plate and silver to create new coins.

The Royalists were here because those nasty, naughty Parliamentarians under Oliver Cromwell were trying to bring accountability into public life and had chased the king out of London. To make matters worse, this Royalist Oxford Parliament wasn't the only one taking place in the country. It was a rival to Cromwell's back in London.

It was not a good time to visit Oxford. Human and animal waste filled the streets. Typhus was killing 40 people a week. In December 1643, Charles I issued a proclamation from the city noting how with 'due consideration of the miseries of this Kingdom, all our good Subjects are no longer to be misled by the Votes, Orders and pretended Ordinances of one or Both Houses of Parliament, which appear by Force and Violence'. Full of magnanimity, Charles promised a 'free and Generall Pardon to anyone who had justly incurred Our displeasure by submitting to, or concurring in unlawfull actions' – if they presented themselves to him personally at Oxford by 22 January, 1644. Oxford was besieged by Parliament three times during the Civil War. That same year, two large armies surrounded the city, but Charles I escaped. Five years and seven days later the king lost his head.

Address Convocation House, Broad Street OX1 3BG | **Getting there** Bus 3, 3A, 6 or 8; the area is a 10- to 15-minute walk east from Oxford Station | **Hours** Viewable from the outside only (unless you want to book it for a wedding or civil partnership ceremony) | **Tip** Time for a swift half after all that English Civil War ruminating in the tiny 16th-century White Horse pub squeezed between Blackwell's main shop and its newer small shop to the west.

34 Enter Balliol College

Bloody Hypocrites

Future PMs Asquith, Macmillan, Heath and Boris, and the sex trafficker Ghislaine Maxwell are among those who have entered the main gates into Balliol, one of Oxford's most celebrated colleges.

A surprise entrant in March 1924 was a tipsy young nun. The porter thought this most odd, given that Balliol was a men-only institution. Quickly, the holy lady was defrocked and turned out to be the son of the bursar, heading back after a raucous party thrown by the Hypocrites' Club. The Hypocrites were a salacious college outfit rumoured to eat new-born babies boiled in wine. Members included Anthony Powell, who went on to write the 12-volume *A Dance to the Music of Time* (1951–75), and the legendary journalist Claud Cockburn, whose motto was 'believe nothing until it has been officially denied'.

The college claims to be the oldest in Oxford. It was founded in 1263 by a John de Balliol, Lord of Barnard Castle, as punishment for insulting the Bishop of Durham. In 1640 a Greek student, Nathaniel Canopius, was possibly the first person in Britain to drink coffee. This frontage on Broad Street was superbly refaced in 1877 by Alfred Waterhouse, but mocked as the 'Broad Street Hotel', a quip complemented by Oscar Wilde, who added: 'C'est magnifique, mais ce n'est pas la gare'.

In summer 2019, Balliol students unsuccessfully staged a campaign to ban new PM Boris Johnson from Balliol for suspending Parliament over Brexit. More excitingly, in June 2014, the plug was pulled at the college disco halfway through Robin Thicke's controversial song 'Blurred Lines' and the DJ was led away by porters. It is not known whether security were objecting to the song's lyrics, which have been cited as promoting rape culture, or because the porters were friends of the late Marvin Gaye whose estate soon received $5 million from Thicke and his associates for over-zealously copying one of his songs.

Address Broad Street OX1 3BJ, +44 (0)1865 277777, www.balliol.ox.ac.uk | Getting there Bus 6 or 13; a 10-minute walk east from Oxford Station | Hours Façade accessible 24 hours; visitors welcome but times restricted (see website) | Tip Fancy reading Greats at Balliol like Boris? Swot up at the excellent huge Waterstone's store on the corner of Broad and Cornmarket Street.

35 Examination Schools

A white sport coat and a pink carnation

You don't have to be a third-year student taking a degree in Greats (that's the course Boris Johnson took at Oxford 1983–86. It wasn't about him, but the Classics) to admire the magnificent awe-inspiring, jaw-dropping architecture of the façade of the Examination Schools. Thomas Graham Jackson completed the work in 1882 in Clipsham stone in the style of a Jacobean mansion, as Oxford needed something suitably grave and glorious.

When a new student arrives at Oxford they are given a thick grey book containing the University's extensive exam rules, a book they never read. A pity really because if they did, they would discover that if you arrive for an exam on a horse in full armour carrying a sword the examiners are obliged to give you a glass of sherry. One student tried this, sidled up on his steed, was offered the tipple, but was then fined a shilling for failing to remember the sword. Another really clever student asked the proctor to bring him Cakes and Ale, victuals rather than the classic Somerset Maugham novel, producing a copy of a 400-year-old law in Latin.

More prosaically, students have to wear precise mufti known as *sub fusc*, plus mortarboard, which must be carried into every exam, but not worn. Then we get to the flowers, usually bought from Oxford's Covered Market. For a first exam, a white carnation usually pinned to gown, pink carnations for interim exams, and a red carnation signalling finals.

And when all the exams are over, the trashing begins. The victim, sorry student, leaves by the back door only to find their friends dousing them in an unholy mixture of glitter, Prosecco, custard and foam. The foolhardy then go and jump in the river, of which Oxford has a huge choice, while some are tied to a tree and covered in unmentionables. Strange and surprising? Vital for those who will soon be running the country.

Address 75–81 High Street OX1 4BG | **Getting there** Bus 3, 3A, 8 or 10; the western end is a 12-minute walk from Oxford Station | **Hours** Viewable from the outside only | **Tip** Next door to the east is the Ruskin School of Fine Art, giving the *flâneur* the opportunity to look up the life and ideas of John Ruskin, the greatest influence on art, architecture and design in Victorian Britain.

36 Faringdon Folly

Okay, if you must

It's the early 1930s and day after day Gerald Hugh Tyrwhitt-Wilson, Lord Berners to underlings, goes for his constitutional around Faringdon Hill in west Oxfordshire. One day during his excursion, he flippantly remarks to his companion, Robert Heber-Percy, an actor known as 'the Mad Boy', that 'this Hill needs a Tower'. They draw up the plan and go to the council. When members ask what purpose will be served by the structure, the good lord, who must be reading Jorge Luis Borges, replies: 'The great point of the Tower is that it will be entirely useless'.

The council in a rare moment of bonhomie said, okay then, go ahead, as long as it only exceeds the height of the tallest local trees by three feet. All 100 feet of Faringdon Folly appeared in 1935. Lord Berners 'gave' it to Heber-Percy as a birthday present, but the latter wasn't impressed. Nevertheless, Faringdon has been hailed as 'Britain's finest 20th-century folly… one of the most important in Britain'.

A late 18th-century local was Henry Pye, who would walk to the top of Faringdon Hill every day carrying a sapling of Scots Pine in support of the Jacobites, the Scots who wanted to be back on the British throne in place of the German Georgians. Pye was Poet Laureate 1790–1813, and has been described as the worst holder of that title that has ever been. His birthday ode to George III was so awful a critic lampooned it with the line 'four and twenty blackbirds, baked in a pie' – Henry Pye. The poet planted a pine copse that was almost destroyed in 1919 when the council sold the plot to a timber merchant – until Lord Berners stepped in to save it.

Faringdon Hill offers clear views across the Thames Valley. Long gone, though, is Faringdon Castle, which Robert Earl of Gloucester built to support Matilda's campaign to depose Stephen as king of England in the 12th century.

Address Folly Path, Faringdon SN7 7AQ | Getting there By car, take the A 420 to the village – you can't miss the folly. It is not possible to drive right up to the Tower, so you'll need to park along Stanford Road (a five-minute walk from the Tower). | Hours Folly woodland area accessible 24 hours; Tower open Apr–Oct 1st & 3rd Sundays | Tip A mile or so to the south-west is the Great Coxwell Barn, the only surviving remnant of a 13th-century grange that provided income to Beaulieu Abbey.

37 First Ever Oxfam Shop

Faith, shop and charity

When a group of Quakers and local academics led by a Cecil Jackson-Cole formed the Oxford Committee for Famine Relief and opened a charity shop here in 1947, who could have predicted that it would become a global giant and a British institution famed for purveying undrinkable fair trade coffee, DVDs of films no one wants to watch, and men's shirts no one wants to wear? – Oxfam.

Four years earlier, volunteers had set up a temporary gift shop in a local department store, and thousands was raised for starving people in Greece. One of their first campaigns was to get the British government to change its policy and allow food imports into war-ravaged Germany under the jurisdiction of the Red Cross. The Oxford committee took the initiative, pledging to relieve 'suffering arising as a result of wars or other causes in any part of the world'.

When Leslie Kirkley became General Secretary in 1951, he began a 24-year job of transforming the organisation from a local charity into a world-renowned aid agency. Its first overseas mission was to tackle famine in Bihar, India. Africa was reached for the first time in the mid-1950s.

It wasn't until 1964 that the name Oxfam officially replaced the Oxford Committee for Famine Relief. That year, an Oxford student decided to raise a million pounds for the charity by inviting the Beatles, then at the height of Beatlemania, to Brasenose College. Who could possibly have the self-confidence and ego for so ambitious a venture? Only a young Jeffrey Archer.

Not quite as spectacular was a 2002 concert in aid of Oxfam's Make Trade Fair campaign held at London's Astoria, starring Chris Martin and Johnny Buckland from ultra-worthy band Coldplay, and incongruously Noel Gallagher. These days, more than 23,000 volunteers run 560 shops nationwide, and they still can't get rid of those 1931 Ordnance Survey maps of Chat Moss bog.

Address 17 Broad Street OX1 3AS, +44 (0)1865 241333 | Getting there Bus 6 or 13; a 10-minute walk east from Oxford Station | Hours Mon – Sat 9.30am – 5.30pm, Sun 11am – 5pm | Tip Head west to St Giles and what must surely be the best-stocked Oxfam bookshop in the universe.

38_First Four-Minute Mile
Race for the prize

Feats of superhuman endurance. Swimming the Channel from Dover to Calais dodging the migrant boats; listening to Iggy Pop's 'L. A. Blues' all the way through; staying awake through an entire TV parliamentary debate; and running the mile (sorry 1,609 metres in Eurospeak), in under four minutes.

No one will ever do it, detractors swore, but on 6 May, 1954, Roger Bannister, a 25-year-old doctor, ex-Exeter and Merton Colleges, achieved the near impossible in 3 minutes 59.4 seconds. What a day he had! He started off at his hospital in London, sharpening his racing spikes with graphite so that they would not pick up too much cinder ash, and made his way to Paddington to get the train to Oxford. The race that took place here off Iffley Road, just south of Magdalen, now the Roger Bannister Running Track, was a competition between the British Athletics team and Oxford University, and it was watched by 3,000 spectators who had been braced for the great event. Fortunately, the wind dropped just before the race started at 6pm. Bannister was helped by his pacers, Christopher Chataway, later a Tory Minister for Posts and Telecommunications, and Chris Brasher, who won the steeplechase gold at the Melbourne Olympics two years later.

To add to the drama, the race was broadcast live on the wireless with commentary from the legendary Harold Abrahams, 1924 Olympic 100 metres champion and hero of the classic British film *Chariots of Fire*. It took only 46 days for Bannister's record to be broken, and this century it's even been shortened by 17 seconds, thanks probably to Shredded Wheat and Guinness. Back in Oxford of 1954, the stadium announcer, who teased the crowd by delaying the announcement of Bannister's race time for as long as possible, was another future celebrity – Norris McWhirter – eventual compiler of the *Guinness Book of Records*. Handy that.

Address Iffley Road Sports Centre, Iffley Road OX4 1EQ, +44 (0)1865 611476 | Getting there The track is on the west side of Iffley Road, the A 4158, opposite Stockmore Street | Hours Mon–Fri 6am–10.30pm, Sat & Sun 7.30am–7.30pm | Tip Nearby, at Nos. 58–60 Iffley Road, is the Christ Church cricket ground where Don Bradman played for Australia against Oxford University in May 1934.

39 Freud's

Psychoanalyse your way to the bar

Surely it's a church, even if it is built to look like a pagan Greek temple with its ionic portico and fluted columns, situated opposite Oxford University Press. No, it's a café-bar, promoted as a 'happening cocktail bar with a European menu' (read: garlic in the sausages and sourdough bread). It used to be St Paul's Church, and was built to offer solace to the public after a cholera bout. With that disease banished, the church closed in the 1960s, was deconsecrated, and bought by the local arts council. In 1988 it was saved from being demolished when it was acquired by David Freud, a graduate of the Courtauld Institute of Art. Freud was fascinated by his father's stories about the atmosphere of mid-20th-century coffee houses in Vienna; where else in Britain could such ambience be re-created, but in Oxford? You can tell it's an intellectual gaff: there are Pre-Raphaelite-styled stained-glass windows and above the main entrance the name is written in Roman style capitals as 'Frevd'.

In 2015, there was a bit of a family row. Freud's 92-year-old mother Iris died. David Freud wanted her buried in the Jewish manner, in a consecrated graveyard, where 'her burial will not be disturbed for hundreds of years', but his sister, Susanna Levrant, insisted on a Church of England ceremony with music. While all these shenanigans were going on, Iris' body was kept in storage for weeks, thus instantly nullifying the Jewish stipulation that a corpse be buried within 24 hours of death.

A judge intervened, inspired by the mediating wisdom of King Solomon, and a compromise was reached: a ceremony would take place in two parts. The first portion would be traditional. Then David Freud and his family would leave before the other branch of the family returned to the chapel to sing 'If You Were the Only Girl in the World'. What would old Sigmund make of it all?

Address 119 Walton Street OX2 6AH, +44 (0)1865 311171, www.freud.eu | Getting there Bus 6 or S2; a 10-minute walk from Oxford Station | Hours Mon–Wed 4–10pm, Thu 4pm–midnight, Fri 4pm–2am, Sat 2pm–2am, Sun 2–10pm | Tip Try the Jude the Obscure pub further along Walton Street, probably not Thomas Hardy's local while he was writing the late Victorian novel of the same name.

40 George Harrison's House
Not all things must pass

George Harrison was clearly the greatest Beatle of all. In 1967, while Paul McCartney could only offer 'Penny Lane', and John Lennon the tedious 'Strawberry Fields Forever', George Harrison came up with the mesmerising and mysterious, entrancing and ethereal 'Within You, Without You', the golden moment on *Sergeant Pepper*, on which he played sitar.

Sadly, the Lennon and McCartney spoilsports would only allow George one or two songs per album. The first they let him include, on the Beatles' second album, *With the Beatles*, was a masterpiece – 'Don't Bother Me' – to which the group dance in an exciting scene from the *Hard Day's Night* film. His 'Think for Yourself' drove the disappointing *Rubber Soul* album along. 'While My Guitar Gently Weeps' was a highlight on the *White Album* and 'Something' from *Abbey Road* gave the Beatles their greatest single. When it came to going solo, George released the sprawling triple album *All Things Must Pass* in 1970, which began with the gorgeous tear-inducing 'I'd Have You Anytime', followed by the joyous Hare Krishna paean 'My Sweet Lord'.

George Harrison bought the Gothic fantasy mansion of Friar Park in 1970. The 62-acre property and estate was built in 1889 by Sir Frank Crisp, a late Victorian eccentric and manic microscope fanatic. Within are caves, grottoes, tunnels, a glut of garden gnomes and an Alpine rock garden. The papers claim there are 120 rooms. Once George's music muse had waned, he got into films and put the house up for collateral to fund Monty Python's classic Biblical tribute *Life of Brian*, mostly simply because he wanted to see it. Python Eric Idle described George's decision as 'the most expensive cinema ticket in movie history'. George Harrison died of lung cancer aged only 58 in 2001. His final words were: 'everything else can wait, but the search for God cannot wait, and love one another'.

Address Friar Park, 65 Crisp Road, Henley-on-Thames RG9 2HL | Getting there The estate is west of the A 4130, just past Waitrose | Hours The estate is viewable from the outside only | Tip Explore Henley itself, a most sumptuous and picturesque Thames-side town.

41 George Michael's House
A different corner

Last Christmas you may have given someone your heart. Next Christmas, you could always try to give them, metaphorically, George Michael's arts and craftsy des res where he died, with remarkable irony, on Christmas Day (2016).

George Michael found fame in the early 1980s in pop duo Wham! At the height of their fame, they split because George wanted to be taken seriously as a profound and philosophical singer, a kind of Home Counties Bruce Springsteen. The Wham! Man bought the riverside property in 2001. Although it's called Mill Cottage, it's a little bigger than yer average Oxfordshire farm worker's bolt hole and was recently sold for £3.4 million. The house was featured on the Oprah Winfrey Show in 2004, during which the singer told viewers: 'This is a 16th-century house that I bought about three years ago and did up myself. It's about as English as you can get. We kept all the original beams. This fire place is original', and then somewhat incongruously added, 'It has a really low ceiling because people were so short in those days'. For equally well-known neighbours, George could cite Jeremy Paxman and Mary Berry.

George Michael was found dead in his bathroom by his partner, Fadi Fawaz, the cause of death later confirmed as heart and liver disease. The bulk of his estate of nearly £100 million was left to his sisters, Melanie and Yioda, but when the family announced they were going to sell the property, fans drew up a petition urging them to turn it into a museum, which never came off. However, each year, fans make the pilgrimage to the house on his birthday, 25 June, to pay their respects. A few years ago, George's housekeeper was probed by his family's lawyers over claims she let ghoulish fans tour his home, which is why the owners have stepped up security in a bid to keep ghoulish fans away. George's family urge fans not to leave floral tributes outside.

Address Mill Cottage, Lock Approach, Goring-on-Thames RG8 9AD | Getting there By car, take the B 4009 to the Thames | Hours Accessible from the outside 24 hours, but respect the owners' privacy | Tip Sup at the Miller of Mansfield pub in the village where George had his own regular table.

42 George Orwell's Grave
Down but not out

He was the greatest British writer of the 20th century. Try reading *Down and Out in Paris and London* (1933) and *Keep the Aspidistra Flying* (1936). Or take the opening of *Coming Up for Air* (1939): 'The idea really came to me the day I got my new false teeth.' The public is better acquainted with *Animal Farm*, wrongly seen originally as a children's book but which finally nailed communism, and *1984*, erroneously cited as a warning of a dystopian, nightmarish surveillance-mad society, but in reality partly a religious parable and partly a satirical dig at the Labour government that was in power the year it was written, 1948.

Yet George Orwell is buried in this low-key grave in All Saints' Church, which surprises those who would expect to find him in a major London cemetery such as Kensal Green or indeed Westminster Abbey. Orwell, real name Eric Blair, had few connections with the area, but his friend, David Astor, editor of the *Observer*, did and he took charge of the dying writer's affairs in 1950. Orwell's wish was for Astor to arrange the burial, which took place on 26 January, 'according to the rites of the Church of England' in the nearest grave to where he died. Orwell died in the Middlesex Hospital, London, but they could find no space in local graveyards – not even the nearest, Old St Pancras, where Victorian author Thomas Hardy was a gravedigger. A Christian burial was a surprise, for Orwell was a self-confessed atheist who had spent his writing career lampooning the Church, particularly in *1984*.

Orwell's gravestone is also surprisingly understated. It simply says: 'Here lies Eric Arthur Blair…' There is no mention of his alter ego or his work. But then he was no Rothschild when it came to the wallet stakes and he had deliberately underplayed his upper middle-class background – Eton, a spell in the Colonies – to spend so much of his life documenting the poor, and occasionally becoming one of them, in search of inner salvation and good copy.

Address All Saints Lane, Sutton Courtenay OX14 4AE | Getting there By car, leave the A34 at Drayton and head east; by train to Culham Station and head west | Hours Best in daylight hours | Tip Didcot Railway Centre, a few miles south-east, is a must for train enthusiasts.

43 — Glorious North Oxford

Gateway to suburban heaven

Here, a couple of miles north of the burger smells of Cornmarket, is an idyllic enclave in the most idyllic of cities that stretches from the canal in the west to the River Cherwell in the east. This is the Oxford of 'spacious and quiet streets, autumnal mists, grey springtime, glory of her summer days when the bells ring out high and clear over her gables and cupolas, exhaling the soft airs of centuries of youth', as Evelyn Waugh put it in *Brideshead Revisited*.

But no one has explained it better than D. W. Riley in his 'Expansion of Towns – Planned and Unplanned' from 1957. 'Gothic, gabled, red brick villas. Tree-lined, mature gardens brimming with lilac and forsythia, copper beech and apple blossom. Mellow gravel drives of yellowing local stone, wisteria-clad eaves and laurel green drainpipes.'

Hey, it's so magnificent, only Richmond Hill can beat it.

Here are schools with waiting lists stretching all the way north to Banbury, particularly the phantasmagorically named Dragon School, not a school for dragons but Alma Mater to the lovable 20th-century poet John Betjeman and the brilliantly intrepid late journalist Christopher Booker... They don't like to be reminded that the useless police chief Cressida Dick also attended. Fittingly, there is a Christian college called Wycliffe Hall, named after John Wycliffe (1328–84), one of the greatest ever Britons, the first cleric to challenge the power of the Romish church, whose bones were ground down to dust on the order of Pope Martin V for the 'crime' of translating the Bible into English.

This enclave is the very epitome of middle-class aspiration, and what more formidable a symbol of grandiosity can there be than Samuel Lipscomb Seckham's classical-styled arch of 1855 on the road Park Town, framed by a tangle of dark green trees known as the Jungle?

Address Park Town OX2 6SH | **Getting there** Bus 6 or 423 | **Hours** Accessible 24 hours |
Tip After all that glorious town architecture, relax, wine and dine at the Cherwell Boathouse
on Bardwell Road and play on your phone the obvious Eno song: 'Backwater, we're sailing at
the edges of time'.

44 Grand Café
'Crème tangerine and Montelimar'

This opulent Parisian-styled chic café is perfectly situated. It stands on the site of England's first coffee house, which was opened in 1652 by Jacob, a Jewish entrepreneur. Jacob's gaff was described in Anthony Wood's Antiquary of Oxford as a 'coffey house at the Angel in the parish of S. Peter… and there it was by some, who delighted in noveltie, drank'. These cafés were where locals could discover what was happening in the world – that was until Charles II banned the joints in 1675 because patrons were using them to spread 'diverse False, Malitious and Scandalous Reports to the Defamation of His Majesties Government and to the Disturbance of the Peace and Quiet of the Realm'.

In the 18th century, Oxford found a new exotic foreign delicacy: chocolate, especially hot chocolate, which was then flavoured with spices and cinnamon. Coffee and chocolate were considered to be health drinks and sold at apothecaries. Such was the beginning of what today is a multi-million pound industry, with most of the British population spending vast amounts of money on invigorating, awakening caffeine-based concoctions while others for unknown reasons *pur-chase* flat whites.

The Grand Café opened here in 1997. By then, the building had amassed a most colourful history. It had been an inn, hotel, grocers, Co-op and post office. The Inn was the Angel, Oxford's most important late 18th-century coaching terminus, where 10 coaches would start out for London each day at 8am. Even the legendary Oxford Tube doesn't often match that. Royalty loved staying at the Angel, for instance Christian II of Denmark in 1768 and Queen Adelaide, consort to William IV, in 1835. Now, the glitterati and maybe a royal or two in disguise, arrive for cream teas and high teas amid the opulence of the marble-pillared, historic gold-leafed building. In the evening the building is available for private hire; minimum 20 people.

Address 84 High Street OX1 4BG, +44 (0)1865 204463, www.thegrandcafe.co.uk | Getting there Bus 3, 3A, 8 or 10; the western end is a 12-minute walk from Oxford Station | Hours Mon–Thu 9am–6.30pm, Fri–Sun 9am–7pm | Tip The Queen's Lane Coffee House on the opposite side of the road claims to be the oldest continually working coffee house in Europe, having opened in 1654. More prosaically it has only been on the present site since 1970.

45 The Greatest Rowers
Statues fit for Olympians

Steve Redgrave and Matthew Pinsent were no ordinary Olympians. Redgrave, born in nearby Marlow, is the only sportsman to have won gold at five successive Games. He carried the British flag at two Olympic opening ceremonies and even managed to make it to No. 36 in the BBC poll of the 100 Greatest Britons. (Guess which war-time PM made No. 1.) And that's despite suffering from ulcerative colitis and diabetes mellitus type 2.

After winning the 1996 gold, Britain's only one in Atlanta, Redgrave stated that if anyone found him close to a rowing boat again they could shoot him. He was probably joking, for he resumed training after a four-month break. When Redgrave won again in 2000, he retired. For more than two decades he had also taken part in the Henley Regatta, winning a host of medals. This century he has received the OBE and a Knighthood.

Matthew Pinsent, from Norfolk, won 10 world championship gold medals, including the 1991 event with Redgrave. Further success followed at the 1992 and 1996 Olympics. In 2000 he won Olympic gold as part of the legendary coxless four team with James Cracknell and Tim Foster, as well as Redgrave, as usual. At one time he enjoyed the largest lung capacity recorded for any sportsman at 8.5 litres.

Sean Henry's *Rowers* weighs a third of a ton, and the figures are just larger than the men's real life sizes. They are situated in the River & Rowing Museum by the Thames, where Redgrave and Pinsent spent so much time training. It is only appropriate that they are located in Henley, the home of British rowing and a town best known for its famous regatta. The Henley Regatta was established in 1839 and lasts for six days early in July. It is an essential part of the English social season that starts with Cheltenham in March and includes the Boat Race, the Chelsea Flower Show, Royal Ascot, the Lord's Test and ends with Goodwood in September.

Address Henley-on-Thames RG9 1BF | **Getting there** The statues and the museum are a few minutes south-east from Henley Station; by road, take the A 4155 to Quebec Road and head east | **Hours** Accessible 24 hours | **Tip** Henley Bridge sports some formidable carvings. The one facing upstream is of Isis, the name of the Thames in Oxford, and the one facing downstream is Tamesis, or Old Father Thames.

46 Harris' Towering DIY
Perfection or pastiche?

Debate will rage for ever over how Oxford should continue to be built. Respec' to the glories of the past, to the presence of the greatest of British architects, Wren and Hawksmoor, or bold imaginative experimental ideas that shriek of now?! For Harris Manchester, the college that most people think is in the Oasis city of the North West rather than in Oxford, the answer is style and elegance. Nevertheless, Harris received flack in 2014 when the Siew-Sngiem clock tower and Sukum Navapan gate went up. Not because the name was too long to fit into a tweet, but because the design was considered a little too traditional, too reactionary, too olde-worlde. One critic went as far as damning the new creation as 'sad retro pastiche, as usual in Oxford, with its deep fear of the modern age. Poundbury for the donnish classes', referring to King Charles' pastiche Dorset village.

Why the college's unusual name? Harris Manchester was founded in Warrington in 1757 as a college for Unitarians – basically one love, one Jah, one i-nity – where one of the teachers included Joseph Priestley who discovered oxygen, and the nastier carbon monoxide and ammonia. It moved to Manchester in 1786, where its leading figure was the remarkable John Dalton, creator of atomic theory that changed the world.

Probably due to its non-conformist stance, the college embraced radical ideas such as the abolition of slavery, and even allowed women to attend lectures in the 1870s. As the Manchester Academy, it moved to Oxford in 1893, and in 1901 one of its first graduates, Gertrude von Petzold, became the first woman minister in England – for the Unitarian Church. During World War II, the government requisitioned the college buildings to plan Operation Overlord, or the D-Day landings. Manchester joined the university in 1996, taking its new name from a donation by Lord Harris of Peckham.

Address Mansfield Road OX1 3TD | Getting there Bus 3, 3A, 8 or 10; a 20-minute walk from Oxford Station | Hours Accessible from the outside only | Tip For further non-conformist architecture, head north to Mansfield College (www.mansfield.ox.ac.uk).

47 Headington Shark

Don't go near the roof!

It's one of the most bizarre animalian sculptures in the country. *Jaws* devotees come from all over the world to New High Street, Headington, a couple of miles east of Oxford city centre, to check whether it's really true that the tail of a 26-foot fibreglass shark is sticking out of the roof of a normal house.

The shark first jumped out of the water (possibly the Thames, possibly somewhere off Australia) in August 1986. Bill Heine, an Oxford journalist, came up with the idea while sitting on the door-step of the house chatting with designer John Buckley over a glass of wine. Buckley designed it and Anton Castiau, a local carpenter, built it. Originally it was given the name *Untitled 1986*, which hardly did the beast justice.

Inspiration also came as a statement against American warplanes flying from the nearby Upper Heyford air base to bomb Libya in retaliation for terrorist attacks on American troops. With the shark, Heine was making a statement not only against that round of bombing, but against atomic weapons in general. It was appropriately unveiled on the 41st anniversary of the dropping of the A Bomb on Nagasaki in 1986. According to Heine, 'The shark was to express someone feeling totally impotent and ripping a hole in their roof out of a sense of impotence and anger and desperation. It is saying something about CND, nuclear power, Chernobyl and Nagasaki.'

Oxford Council wasn't keen and threatened to have it taken down for flouting planning rules. They felt the shark wasn't in keeping with the elegance and sophistication of one of the world's most prestigious cities, and ordered it back in the ocean. However, in 2022 they did an about swim and decided to grant the beast heritage status for its 'special contribution' to the community. In 2016, Heine's son Magnus bought the house to preserve the shark and has since run it as an Airbnb guesthouse.

Address 2 New High Street, Headington OX3 7AQ | Getting there Bus 8; the shark is just off the A 420 | Hours Accessible 24 hours | Tip Visit the less dangerous C. S. Lewis home, the Kilns, a mile east, where he wrote all his Narnia books.

48 Hell's Passage

Birthplace of the muse

Human and canine filth running down the road. Piles of rotting rubbish heaped up on the street. Cut-throats and ne'er-do-wells hiding in wait at every corner. No wonder they called it Hell's Passage. Yet from this rendezvous of repugnance comes a story of aspiration and acceptance. Jane Burden was born here in poverty in 1839. The daughter of a stableman and an illiterate domestic servant, she was lucky (?) enough to be picked up at a lowdown Oxford music hall by William Morris, the towering intellectual of the mid-19th century, and his almost equally gifted artist associate Edward Burne-Jones. The pair asked her to pose as Guinevere for an Arthurian mural they were painting in the Oxford Union.

Maybe it was the emolument that was dangled in front of Jane that persuaded her? She accepted and became a sophisticate who played the piano, and spoke French and Italian. She is believed to be the model for Eliza Doolittle in George Bernard Shaw's *Pygmalion*, which later became *My Fair Lady*. Morris eventually married her, but it was not a simple match. Dante Gabriel Rossetti, the flamboyant Pre-Raphaelite artist, fell in love with Jane and made her his muse. The love triangle raged for many years in an unconventional ménage-à-trois at Kelmscott Manor in west Oxfordshire. Such labyrinthine romantic collusions!

Jane Burden can be seen in many well-known paintings of the period, including Rossetti's famous *Proserpine* of 1874, reproduced in a thousand prints and place mats, which personified the idea of the Victorian ideal of feminine beauty – pursed rosebud lips, long flowing dark hair, one shoulder exposed. Eventually this pose became unfashionable and the paintings that featured them were attacked early in the 20th century by the suffragettes.

Hell's Passage is cleaned up now as the blander St Helen's Passage and there is a blue plaque marking Jane Burden's birthplace.

Address St Helen's Passage, off New College Lane OX1 3SU | Getting there Bus 3, 3A, 8 or 10; a 20-minute walk from Oxford Station | Hours Accessible 24 hours | Tip At 7 New College Lane there's a plaque to Edmond Halley, the early 18th-century astronomer who gave his name to the most famous comet in the universe, due back in 2061. Don't miss it.

49 Here James Sadler Went Up

Full of hot air

It's the morning of 4 October, 1784 and 31-year-old pastry chef James Sadler decides to do something nobody has done before: set off up into the sky in a hydrogen balloon. Sadler went up from Deadman's Walk, and eventually came down five miles away near Woodeaton. He calculated he'd made 3,600 feet in 30 minutes, earning his place in the record books as England's first aeronaut. Sadler wrote about his amazing feat in suitably 18th-century purple prose: 'I perceived no Inconvenience, and being disengaged from all terrestrial Things, contemplated a most charming distant View. With Pleasure and Admiration I beheld the Surface of the Earth like a large and extensive Plain, and felt myself perfectly agreeable.' He became an instant hero in Oxford. 'The townspeople pulled his carriage all around Oxford for hours,' his biographer Richard O. Smith recorded. National fame followed and huge crowds arrived for later lift-offs. Hot air balloon hysteria swept the country. The *Daily Chronicle* waxed how 'Sadler is known from the humble cabbage seller to the mightiest of lords'.

Like a later Oxford balloonist, Richard Branson, Sadler had other great skills, but unlike Branson they never brought him riches. He experimented on air pumps and in distilling seawater. He patented a 32-pounder gun for the Navy that wowed Admiral Nelson: 'I would take on board the *Victory* as many guns as Mr Sadler could send alongside,' the great warrior declared in the run-up to Trafalgar, 1805. Sadler's son Windham ballooned up from Hyde Park for the centenary of the Hanoverians' usurping of the British Crown in 1814, but died in a ballooning accident 10 years later.

James Sadler died on 28 March, 1828 and was buried at St Peter-in-the-East. There are two other plaques to Sadler in Oxford: one in St Edmund Hall library and one on the Town Hall.

James Sadler
1753 ~ 1828
First English Aeronaut
who in a fire balloon
made a successful
ascent from near this
place ~ 4th October 1784
to land near Woodeaton

Address Deadman's Walk OX1 4JF | Getting there Bus 3, 3A, 8 or 10; a 12-minute walk from Oxford Station | Hours Accessible 24 hours | Tip Come down to earth to visit nearby Corpus Christi College, responsible for devising the King James Bible, the most popular book in the history of the English language (www.ccc.ox.ac.uk).

50 Hill Hall Horror

Maxwell House – it's time to smell the coffee

For around 150 years, Headington Hill Hall was simply a grand aristocratic Italianate mansion on the edge of town, looking down on the *hoi-polloi*. It was built for Oxfordshire brewers the Morrells, and started off small-scale, but by 1858 sported 51 rooms tended by 19 servants. Oscar Wilde was dressed as Prince Rupert when he attended a fancy dress ball here in 1878.

In 1953 James Morrell III sold the hall to Oxford City Council. Then disaster struck. It was leased by the monstrous megalomaniac publisher and one-time Labour MP Robert Maxwell, he who later robbed his own Mirror Group pension fund. Cap'n Bob restored it, installing a 150-year-old chimney piece ripped out of his offices in Georgian Fitzroy Square. For a few years Robert Maxwell was a hero in Oxford. In 1982, he saved local football club Oxford United, new to the League, from bankruptcy, but soon re-emerged as a villain when he proposed merging the club with nearby rivals Reading into Thames Valley Royals. Protests saw it off. Somehow – no one can explain it – Oxford United made it into the top division and stunned the world of football by winning the League Cup in 1986.

At the same time his favourite daughter, Ghislaine, later to find fame as a sex trafficker, entered Oxford University. Every day she would join the ordinary folk on the bus, heading for Balliol to read modern history. Meanwhile, Maxwell tired of football and turned Headington Hill Hall into a fortress with guards at the main entrance, video cameras and a barbed wire fence. You have to when you're a secret member of Mossad. It didn't stop Maxwell falling off his boat, the *Lady Ghislaine*, ironically, near Gran Canaria in 1991 – or was he pushed? – following which the details of his dreadful crimes emerged. Headington Hill Hall is now part of Oxford Brooks University. The Law Faculty. Sort of makes sense.

Address Headington Hill Hall, Headington Road OX3 0BP | Getting there By car, take Headington Road, the A 420; the hall is to the north, half way between Marston Road and Pullens Lane | Hours Really only for students, but they'll probably let you in if you have a dig at the Maxwells | Tip Head south-east beyond the Eastern By-Pass to glorious Shotover Country Park with its hidden valleys, wildlife habitats and peaceful woodlands.

51 Inklings Pub, Mark 1
The Eagle and Child, aka The Bird and Baby

Lovers of the works of J. R. R. Tolkien and C. S. Lewis arrive from across the literary world to sup in and savour this magnificent historic pub where the two authors and their circle – the Inklings – met every Tuesday morning from 1939 to 1952.

John Ronald Reuel Tolkien is read more, thanks to *The Hobbit* (1937) and *Lord of the Rings* (1954). Tolkien was born in South Africa. At a very young age, he was bitten by a baboon spider which, some say, accounts for his flights of fancy and fantasy. Clive Staples Lewis, best known for *The Chronicles of Narnia* series (1950 – 56), once wrote how his 'happiest hours were spent with three or four old friends in old clothes tramping together and putting up in small pubs'. Lewis' secretary, William Hooper, noted that Lewis was 'a man of robust thirst' who never drank halves. He was mentioned in Edmund Crispin's 1947 detective novel *Swan Song* in which a character notes 'There goes C. S. Lewis. It must be Tuesday'. Here in June 1950 Lewis distributed the proofs for what became the ever-popular *The Lion, The Witch and the Wardrobe* (1950). In 1956, he even got married upstairs, to the poet Joy Gresham, who converted from Judaism to Christianity after reading his books.

The pub has an ancient history. During the English Civil War of the 1640s, the Chancellor of the Exchequer lodged here and paid the Royalist court within. Its name might derive from the story of Ganymede, 'the most beautiful of mortals' in Greek mythology, who was abducted by the eagle of Zeus. A more likely story was that it was taken from the coat of arms of the landowners, the Earls of Derby, and the legend of an aristocrat baby found in an eagle's nest.

The Eagle and Child's closure during Covid was mourned as another example of the imminent collapse of Western civilisation. However, the owners, St John's College, want to reopen it with a boutique hotel attached.

Address 49 St Giles OX1 3LU | Getting there Bus 6 or 13; a 15-minute walk from Oxford Station | Hours Currently viewable from the outside only | Tip Sober reflection time can be experienced at the nearby Oxford War Memorial.

52 Inklings Pub, Mark 2
The Lamb and Flag

What a choice was in store for centuries for the thirsty scholar and intellectual at St Giles. Two legendary literary pubs either side of the wide, imposing main road. And so there was much rejoicing in October 2022 when the Lamb and Flag reopened after a couple of years of Covid-induced closure.

The Lamb and Flag first opened in 1613 and is still suffused with tradition *par excellence*: stone flagged floor, aged fireplace, and a clock that runs backwards showing Theakston's Old Peculier Time, named after that brewer's famous strong ale. There are no TVs, jukebox or fruit machines. The pub is owned by nearby St John's College, and profits from supping are ploughed into students' doctorate scholarships.

The pub has many literary associations. It is where Arabella the barmaid works in Thomas Hardy's 1895 classic *Jude the Obscure*. It was loved by Dylan Thomas… hold on, he loved all pubs. And it was one of two favourites for the Inklings, the group of writers associated with C. S. Lewis and J. R. R. Tolkien. Lewis, responsible for the 1950s series *The Chronicles of Narnia*, lauded the pub's 'golden sessions', filled with scholars' scintillating soliloquies. 'Our slippers were on, our feet spread out towards the blaze and our drinks at our elbows when the whole world opened itself to our minds as we talked…'

More recent cultural events have been weirder. In 2017, new applicants to join Oxford's most élitist toffs' fraternity, the Bullingdon Club, were told to arrive at the Lamb and Flag at 1.30pm dressed in an entirely yellow outfit holding a 'plush squirrel toy', a diamond, and a 'smutty or left-wing publication'. They then had to order five particular drinks, including a pint of champagne, and down them in a predetermined order in front of current members who would monitor their performance. It is not known whether any of them were still alive after the ritual.

Address 12 St Giles OX1 3JS, +44 (0)1865 515787, www.lambandflagthai.com | Getting there Bus 6 or 13; a 15-minute walk from Oxford Station | Hours Sun–Wed 11am–11pm, Thu–Sat 11am–midnight | Tip A short distance to the east is the university's intensely Gothic Museum of Natural History, which also provides the only access to the adjacent Pitt Rivers Museum (www.prm.ox.ac.uk).

53 __Iris Murdoch's Address

The house, the house

A mile and a half north of the city centre is 30 Charlbury Road, one of the great modern-day literary addresses. For here lived the remarkable Iris Murdoch and her less celebrated husband John Bayley. The accolades came fast for Murdoch in the 1950s through novels that tackled themes of good and evil, and the power of the unconscious, as part of a body of literature that created free, independent characters who are not 'merely puppets in the exteriorization of some closely-locked psychological conflict', as one critic put it.

Her first published novel, *Under the Net* (1954), was chosen in 1998 as one of the 100 best English language novels of the 20th century by the Modern Library group. *The Sea, The Sea* won the Booker Prize in 1978. In 2008 *The Times* ranked her 12th on a list of the '50 greatest British writers since 1945'.

Iris Murdoch was born in Dublin in 1919. She entered Somerville College in 1938 to read Greats, one of the legendary Oxford courses whose name befuddles outsiders but simply combines Classics, Ancient History and Philosophy. Murdoch gained a first in 1942 and went to work at the Treasury, before joining the United Nations' Relief and Rehabilitation service working in recently occupied countries in Europe. She then studied philosophy at Cambridge, and in 1948 became a Fellow at Oxford's St Anne's College, while being barred from the US for having joined the Communist Party.

Iris Murdoch believed that imaginative prose was the best medium for focusing attention on the individual because it is '*par excellence* the form of art most concerned with the existence of other persons'. In 1959's *The Sublime and the Good*, she defined love as 'the perception of individuals. Love is the extremely difficult realization that something other than oneself is real', explaining that the main subject of her fiction is love. In *The Bell*, the Abbess tells Michael Meade that 'all of our failures are ultimately failures in love'.

Address 30 Charlbury Road OX2 6UU | Getting there Bus 6 or 423 | Hours Viewable from the outside only | Tip One of Iris Murdoch's favourite Oxford places to wander in was the garden at nearby Lady Margaret Hall, one of the first Oxford colleges (in 1879) to admit women. Or as she put it near the end of *A Fairly Honourable Defeat* (1970), her 13th novel, 'People from a planet without flowers would think we must be mad with joy the whole time to have such things about us'.

54 Jeremy Clarkson's Farm

'My farm is red hot. Your farm ain't doodly-squat'

The flamboyant petrolhead bought a thousand-acre farm on the Sarsden estate in 2008 to give himself a new challenge. He renamed it the Diddly Squat Farm to signify its lack of productivity, but cultivating barley, rapeseed and wheat was not enough for the *Top Gear* host, and he was soon developing the project into a TV programme, released by Amazon Prime in June 2021. In the show, Clarkson is assisted by young local Kaleb Cooper who has barely left the locale, only been to London once, and never made it abroad. Kaleb advises on such vital topics as the technicalities involved in running a tractor. When Clarkson discovered that the relevant government ministry, Defra, required the meadows to be mown annually, he hired a flock of sheep rather than an electric seated lawnmower. He also bought 78 mules and, amazingly, found that they were difficult to control – even with an electric fence.

Clarkson then set up a Diddly Squat farm shop, 'a small barn full of good, no-nonsense things you'll like. We don't for example sell kale' – whatever that is. In February 2023 it was revealed that Clarkson had made only £144 profit the previous year, so he went out and bought a herd of cows that later turned out to be in danger of catching TB from the farm badgers. Perhaps killing the badgers might be a solution? No. This would be illegal. A new wheeze came into his mind – open a restaurant in the barn – but will the council approve? No.

The reaction from local farmers was positive, but naturally the *Guardian* weren't impressed and denounced him as 'a right-wing bully columnist', as opposed to their left-wing bully columnists. And just to attract more viewers, even though his viewing figures came in at more than four million, Jeremy Clarkson then infamously used his newspaper column to 'reach out', as the *Guardian* might say, to Meghan Markle. That didn't go so well.

Address Chipping Norton Road, Chadlington OX7 3PE | **Getting there** By car, take the A 44 to Chipping Norton and head south | **Hours** Farm shop open Thu – Sun 9.30am – 4.30pm | **Tip** Head a mile north-east to Heythrop Zoological Gardens for the kind of wildlife not seen on Clarkson's Farm (www.heythropzoologicalgardens.org).

55 Kellogg College

Where students get their Snap, Crackle and Pop

No, the students at Kellogg College don't start each day with a 'bowl of sunshine'. No, they don't greet each other with a cereal-induced salutation of 'Good morning! Good morning!', as in the famous ad and the Beatles song of the same name. Well, not necessarily so. And no, Tony the Tiger isn't the college principal.

Kellogg College is graduate only. It was founded as the university's 36th college as recently as 1990, first as Rewley House and later renamed after the cereal kings. The original Kelloggs were John Harvey Kellogg and his brother Will Keith Kellogg. They were members of an 1870s Seventh Day Adventist church that practised vegetarianism, exercise, sun-bathing, hydrotherapy, and desisting from smoking, sherbets and nookie. One night, John Kellogg left a batch of wheat-berry dough behind and was surprised to obtain delicate flakes that could then be baked. It was plain special K-ing from there.

Inspiration for the college has come from 19th-century progressive figures who began to take Oxford 'to the masses', giving lectures in town halls, public libraries and village school rooms. The college's aims are mostly post-breakfastist. They run courses on population ageing and support lifelong learning. There is a lack of old-fashioned Oxford formality between Fellows and students, no high table at meals, grace is in Welsh, and it has its own tartan.

But Kellogg hasn't always had the best press when it comes to attracting students. One report on the much-read Student Room website came from a best-not-named freshman who admitted: 'I'm a full-time MPhil in linguistics. Got admitted to Kellogg and did some research into the college, which turns out to be a total disappointment... mostly part-timers, weak atmosphere, virtually no history, stupid name, small site, ugly buildings, expensive meals, away from centre, tiny tiny library, no choir, no chapel, no tradition, no societies'. So no second helpings of raisin bran for him then!

Address 60–62 Banbury Road, Park Town OX2 6PN, +44 (0)1865 612000, www.kellogg.ox.co.uk | Getting there Bus 6 or 13; a 20-minute walk from Oxford Station | Hours Mon–Fri 9am–5pm | Tip You know Oxford is an intellectual place. It has proper bookshops, such as the Last Bookshop, a short distance south-west on Walton Street (www.lastbookshopoxford.com).

56 Lawrence of Arabia Tunnel
His first pillar of wisdom

Many people take out a boat on the River Cherwell by Magdalen Bridge to luxuriate on the water. The young T. E. Lawrence, who lived locally, and went on to become one of Britain's greatest military campaigners as Lawrence of Arabia, preferred to negotiate the treacherous tunnel of the Trill Mill Stream from Hythe Bridge Street to Christ Church Memorial Gardens, a route usually inhabited only by fish and rats, to practise for his archaeological digs.

Lawrence was born in Tremadog, Wales, in 1888. His family moved to Oxford in 1896 and he found in this city inspiration for his growing interest in the Middle Ages. Aged 15, Lawrence cycled around the locale, building up huge stamina and strength, attributes that served him well in campaigns for the British in the desert during the 1914–18 Great War. He visited church after church, making rubbings of the brasses and scouring building sites for curios, which the family presented to Oxford's Ashmolean museum.

T. E. Lawrence was always ingeniously practical. A 1906 photograph shows him and fellow pupils from the local school posing standing and sitting. What is special about the photo is that he took it himself using a bicycle pump under his jacket, linked by rubber tubing to the camera. Lawrence read history at Jesus College, Oxford, 1907–1910. After one summer term he cycled solo through France to the Mediterranean. The next year he set out alone on a three-month walking tour of Crusader castles in Syria, then under Ottoman Empire control, experiences that proved invaluable when he led the Arab revolt against the Turks during the Great War, a major success for the allied war effort. Mystery surrounds Lawrence's death. A motorbike accident in Dorset in 1935 involved an unexplained black car at a time when he was allegedly planning a meeting with Hitler. Many now believe he was eliminated by the secret state.

Address Castle Mill Stream, Hythe Bridge Street OX1 2EP | **Getting there** Bus 4A; Oxford Station is nearby | **Hours** Accessible 24 hours, but don't attempt it! | **Tip** Head north a mile and a bit up the Woodstock Road to 2 Polstead Road, boyhood Lawrence home, before it crumbles away due to neglect. Here the young T. E. would fill the bath with water, throw some coins in, and insist the family fish out the money with their mouths.

57 The 'Liberal Prison'

Castle Mill – almost as bad as Castlemilk

For centuries, those who run Oxford have been trying to ruin it. Let's have a motorway through Christ Church Meadow; let's turn High Street Oxford into High Street Bolton. One of the worst blights is this student estate, Castle Mill, a mile north of the station by the Castle Mill Stream.

Castle Mill looks as if a group of *Offiziellen* from an East German *Ratsversammlung* sent it over with love from the Stasi. Or even worse, the tenements of Castlemilk, Glasgow. The blocks have ruined the view of the Celestial City from Port Meadow. Their existence has been described as like building a 'skyscraper beside Stonehenge'. Protesters, including TV historian Professor Diarmaid MacCulloch, have noted that the buildings 'blot out the unique view of Oxford's Dreaming Spires'. As soon as it went up in 2004, there were campaigns to have it demolished. Too late. Instead, they tinkered with it by screening it with trees and adding living walls. Save Port Meadow campaigners cited this as a 'great step. Port Meadow is for everyone in the city, ruined by the Castle Mill flats', but one councillor claimed that it wouldn't make up for the 'architectural mistake'.

To make matters worse, in March 2013, it was revealed that the council was warned about the threat to the views from Port Meadow and that potential pollution at Castle Mill hadn't even been checked before work began, as was required in the planning permission. That June, Castle Mill was nominated for the 2013 Carbuncle Cup, an annual award for the ugliest building in the UK. Judges described it as 'a deeply unimaginative and impoverished design which would lower the spirits whatever its setting, but on the edge of one of central England's most important and ancient landscapes, an outrage'. All it needs now is for King Charles to appear and denounce the site as a 'monstrous carbuncle on the face of a much-loved friend'.

Address Castle Mill, Roger Dudman Way OX1 1AE | **Getting there** Roger Dudman Way runs north–south right to the west of Oxford Station and the railway | **Hours** Accessible to look at 24 hours, but five minutes should be enough | **Tip** Hop over the railway, metaphorically, to explore the lovely Oxford Canal, maybe all 23 miles north to Banbury.

58 Logic Lane

It doesn't make sense

University College is one of the few academic institutions that has a road running through it – Logic Lane. The alleyway has long been the subject of rows between the towned and the gowned, for when the college, around 100 years ago, wanted to build a bridge across to connect two of its buildings, the council demanded £5 a year rent. University College said 'nay', not because the fiver was beyond their budget, but because they claimed they were simply building on and over their own land, which they had looked after since 1681.

Not good enough! The city councillors reminded the college that since the early 13th-century reign of King John, ownership of all thoroughfares in Oxford belonged to them. To give the college a bit of grief, they removed a hinged post at the High Street end that had stopped carts going about their business. Who could settle the row? The High Court ruled in favour of the college, explaining that the city couldn't prove Logic Lane existed at the time of King John. The bridge went up in October 1905, costing the college £300 and the ratepayers around 10 times that amount in legal fees.

Logic Lane was originally Horseman Lane. It acquired its new name to commemorate medieval bouts between Nominalists (those who believe abstract objects don't really exist; they're just names or labels) and Realists (they do, they do!). Or maybe after a 17th-century school of logicians. There's a plaque to alumnus Christian Cole, who enrolled in 1873 to read Classics and became the first African barrister to practise in English courts. Such was the scarcity of similar figures at Oxford, students used to vie just to catch sight of him. He was so popular that when his financial situation deteriorated after his uncle died, fellow students and even the Master of University College raised money to help him. He died of smallpox in 1885 aged only 33.

Address Logic Lane, off High Street OX1 4EX | Getting there Bus 3, 3A, 8 or 10; a 12-minute walk from Oxford Station | Hours Accessible 24 hours | Tip It would only be logical to head back to High Street and have a peek inside Babylon Trading, one of Oxford's many innovative independent stores.

59 Magdalen Bridge
Don't go near the water!

This beautiful bridge marks the eastern boundary of the city centre bestriding the River Cherwell. Below are boats enticing the visitors and locals to go punting at what is one of the most splendid waterside settings in the country. But in case you think nothing could go wrong, it is here every first of May that large crowds of students gather to watch the hardy and the foolhardy throw themselves off into the drink. Dangerously shallow water level? Threat of injury? Pppffff!

Those who think this may be a tradition dating back to the days when Charles I made Oxford his royalist headquarters should think again. It is a purely 21st-century phenomenon. Throughout April, tense meetings take place between Oxfordshire Ambulance Service, Thames Valley Police and the councils. In the hours leading up to the event, much of Oxford stays up all night, and nightclubs, bars and restaurants that normally close at 2am carry on until six.

Barriers are set up at 3am, and by dawn huge crowds have gathered under Magdalen College tower, listening to the all-male choir, revelling in the Morris dancing, and then preparing for the dowsing and splashing while scores of police and private guards line up on either side of the crossing to stop anyone from plunging.

Does this stop them? Of course not! Despite the security, the first student eventually scales the walls and leaps. In 2001, more than 40 people were injured – the odd broken leg or arm or both – after jumping into the Cherwell. Now the bridge is routinely closed on May Day.

Fortunately, there are more successes than failures. A Fyn Gunn, not even an Oxford student, told the local press that he was 'worried, but just had to jump' as he clambered out of the water dressed in top hat and tails, Jacob Rees-Mogg style. Now there is serious fear that the weight of people might cause the bridge to crumble.

Address Magdalen Bridge OX1 4AU | Getting there Bus 3, 3A, 8 or 10; the western end is a 12-minute walk from Oxford Station | Hours Accessible 24 hours | Tip If it's spring, summer or early autumn, punt! Basically, it's pushing yourself around the waterways with a long metal pole, which ain't easy.

60 Magnificent Magdalen
No need to be maudlin

The college of St Mary Magdalen (pronounced 'maudlin') enjoys one of the most picturesque settings of any in Oxford, standing majestically by the River Cherwell. It was founded in 1458 by William of Waynflete, Bishop of Winchester and Lord Chancellor of England, for the study of theology and philosophy. The square Magdalen tower, begun in 1492, is a major Oxford landmark. An ancient tradition sees the college choir sing from the top of the choir at 6am each May Day as huge crowds gather to watch the hardiest folk jumping from Magdalen Bridge into the water (see ch. 59).

In the 1680s, James II twice tried to force the Fellows to accept his choice of president. When they refused, he demanded that anyone who opposed him be expelled, which caused national outrage. The king was soon forced off the throne anyway. In the 20th century Magdalen was one of the most successful colleges academically, its reputation sealed by the long spell as history lecturer of A. J. P. Taylor who was so popular he had to give his lectures at 8.30am to avoid the room becoming overcrowded.

Unwelcome publicity came in 1999 when Laura Spence, a state pupil from the North-East, was turned down to read medicine. Labour politicians, including future prime minister Gordon Brown, seized on the story as proof of Oxford's discrimination against working-class applicants. She later went to Harvard and Cambridge.

In summer 2021 there was another huge row when members of the college's Middle Common Room, led by an American, voted to remove a portrait of the queen, citing it as a symbol of 'recent colonial history', but surprisingly without providing a cogent argument in favour of an alternative system for appointing a head of state.

Why is Magdalen pronounced 'maudlin'? It derives from the late medieval English name of Maudelen, derived from the Old French Madelaine, for Mary Magdalene.

Address High Street, just west of the Cherwell, OX1 4AU, +44 (0)1865 276000, www.magd.ox.ac.uk | **Getting there** Bus 3, 3A, 8 or 10; the western end is a 12-minute walk from Oxford Station | **Hours** Daily 10am–dusk or 7pm, whichever is earlier, although the college may close during exam weeks so call the Porters' Lodge before visiting | **Tip** There are some gorgeous waterside strolls to be had in this environ, for instance the Water Meadow and the Grove.

61 The Maharajah's Well
'Its hard soft shell shinin' white in one spot, well'

This magnificent canopy, complete with gilded elephant, houses the cast iron machinery of a Victorian well, a gift from an Indian prince to the village of Stoke Row. The well is four feet in diameter, 368 feet deep (about two Nelson's columns), and covered by this ornate domed shelter, made by a foundry in Wallingford.

The entire feature was paid for by Ishree Pershad Naryan Singh, the Maharajah of Benares, for in the early 1860s he met Oxford man Edward Reade, squire in this parish of Ipsden and governor-general of India's United Provinces, who was helping to sink a well in Benares. Reade told the Maharajah that despite England's reputation as a green and pleasant land, where it rains every day, droughts happen in Oxfordshire. In Ipsden, water had to be fetched by hand from miles away. Reade also told Singh of an urchin who had been beaten by his mother for drinking the last water in their house. The woman had then threatened to beat Reade for criticising her.

The Maharajah was moved enough to dig deep to pay for this well at a cost of £353 13s 7d. He also supplied a well-keeper's cottage and a cherry orchard, whose fruit paid for the well's upkeep. It took a year to dig the well by hand through chalk while workmen desperately tried to avoid shifting sands that could cave in the whole thing. It was opened on Queen Victoria's birthday in 1864, only seven years after the violent and horrendous Indian Mutiny, and used for more than 70 years. Prince Philip visited by helicopter to mark its centenary in 1964, during which water from the Ganges was symbolically poured down. In 2008 it was repainted to restore it to its original Victorian glory. On the red brick base of the canopy are painted iron columns that lead to an onion dome and a gilded spear finial. The elephant was added in 1870. The inscription reads: 'GIVEN BY HIS HIGHNESS THE MAHARAJAH OF BENARES 1864'.

SS THE MAHARAJAH

Address Stoke Row, Henley RG9 5QR | Getting there By car, take the B 481 to Highmoor Cross and head west; park at the Village Hall at Stoke Row | Hours Accessible 24 hours | Tip To the north is Nuffield Place, 20th-century home of the philanthropic Lord Nuffield.

62 The Manor

'Plus… tubular bells!'

It is one of the most remarkable pieces of instrumental music in history, up there with John Coltrane's *Giant Steps* and Shostakovich's Fourth symphony. Beautiful, unpredictable, unfathomable, beyond understanding. Mike Oldfield's 1973 masterpiece, *Tubular Bells*, was recorded here at the Manor. Richard Branson bought the 16th-century property after setting up Virgin Records in 1972, at a time when great innovative rock albums were recorded mostly in London at Abbey Road, Trident or Olympic studios. And nothing was more innovative than *Tubular Bells*.

Mike Oldfield was a child prodigy who began writing this when he was 17. At the end of 1972, he came to record at the Manor, playing everything he could find to create *Tubular Bells*. The first few minutes repeat a mesmerising piano theme with an unusual 15/8 time signature that was used as the theme for the film *The Exorcist*. Using a 1966 Fender Telecaster that belonged to Marc Bolan, Oldfield made some 75 overdubs, tinkering with the speed to distort the sound, even making the guitars seem like bagpipes at one point. The theme gradually changes, leading to an unpredictable roll call of each new instrument, a kind of reverse version of Haydn's *Farewell Symphony*, culminating in the arrival of the tubular bells themselves, found by chance after John Cale left them behind. This build-up was accompanied by announcements from manic eccentric Vivian Stanshall in a ridiculously OTT accent sounding like Jacob Rees-Mogg's posher brother.

Side Two's most unusual piece is the 'Caveman' section. It sounds like a troglodyte announcing there's no bison stew left in the Flint-stones' café, and came about after pressure from Branson to make a vocal single. Angered by Branson's suggestion, Oldfield drank half a bottle of Jameson's and, well sloshed, screamed his brains out for 10 minutes, leaving him so hoarse he couldn't speak. It was worth it.

Address Upper Campsfield Road, Jerome Way OX5 1JL | **Getting there** The house is on the A 4095 halfway between the A 44 and the A 4260 | **Hours** Viewable from the outside only, as it's now a private house, but you could try writing to them in advance | **Tip** Where else but the Jolly Boatman on the A 4260, where Mike and his pals gained inspiration for the project?

63 Manor Country House Hotel

Absolutely no manners

It's a sumptuous 11th-century country house hotel, built as a monastery, now with deluxe quarters, landscaped gardens and an inviting pool. What could possibly go wrong?

One night back in 2015, a shabby minibus arrived and out poured a phalanx of Dom Pérignon-swilling Hooray Henrys. A few hours later, according to one report, 'the tablecloth was drenched in red wine and blood; broken plates littered the floor and a young man in a £4,000 suit lay unconscious'.

Were they pillaged by violent thugs? Almost. The Manor had been 'visited' by the notorious Bullingdon Club. 'They walked in here as if they were the Royal Family', recalled waiter John Wood. 'One half were drinking themselves silly, the other half smashing up the crockery.' The damage was only £400, which, being gentlemen, they settled in cash just as the minibus returned to cart them home. Had this bacchanalian boozy bender taken place in the mid-1980s, it might have featured future PMs Dave and Boris, and Chancellor George. No one is saying who *was* there, thanks to the club's strict omertà, but in two decades' time they will be captains of industry, ambassadors and royal celebs.

Is there a political element to these high japes? Well, when Dave became PM in 2010, two Bullers dressed in suits, ties and top hats unfurled a poster on an Oxfordshire polling booth featuring a photo of Cameron that read 'BRITONS, KNOW YOUR PLACE. VOTE ETON – VOTE TORY'. Why did the toffs need to venture so far from their Oxford colleges? Well, they had been banned from everywhere else in Oxford. The Kings Arms showed them the red card after the Bullingdon boys started a fire and smashed an antique mirror. And that was after ignoring the by-law that banned the Bullingdon from holding events within 15 miles of central Oxford in 1894.

Address Northampton Road, Weston-on-the-Green, Bicester OX25 3QL, +44 (0)1869 350621, www.manorhousecountryhotel.com | **Getting there** By car, road A 34 to the B 430; Islip Station is three miles south | **Hours** Normal country hotel hours | **Tip** An appropriate alternative, half a mile south for aspiring politicians, is The Chequers, not the PM's country retreat, but a homely pub.

64 Martyrs' Cross
Burned to death for their Protestant beliefs

An iron cross in the middle of Broad Street marks the spot where the Protestant martyrs Hugh Latimer, Nicholas Ridley and later Thomas Cranmer were burned at the stake in the 1550s after being convicted of heresy.

Latimer and Ridley were executed on 16 October, 1555, and Cranmer on 21 March, 1556. Hugh Latimer, as Bishop of Worcester, had introduced religious reforms that included wanting the Bible to be available in English. When the Protestant king, Edward VI, died in 1553 and was succeeded by his half-sister, Mary Tudor, a Catholic, aka Bloody Mary, Latimer was in trouble. Nicholas Ridley had been private chaplain to Henry VIII and part of the team that compiled England's first *Book of Common Prayer*, a Protestant measure. As he burned, Latimer turned to Ridley and announced: 'Be of good comfort Master Ridley, and play the man. We shall this day light such a candle by God's grace in England as I trust shall never be put out'. Ridley took some time to die, for the packets of gunpowder tied to his body failed to ignite. Thomas Cranmer had to wait till March 1556. He had been Archbishop of Canterbury under Henry VIII and played a major role in the king's annulment of his marriage to Catherine of Aragon. He watched the burning of Ridley and Latimer from the Bocardo prison where he was served wine, figs, oysters, veal and almonds.

After the horrendous burnings, Cranmer recanted his beliefs. But Queen Mary didn't believe him and he went to the flames on 21 March, 1556 announcing: 'I have sinned, in that I signed with my hand what I did not believe with my heart. When the flames are lit, this hand shall be the first to burn'. When the fire began, he leaned forward and held his right hand in the flames until it was charred to a stump. Just once he raised his left hand to wipe his forehead.

Oxford no longer burns heretics. It just cancels them instead.

Address 7 Broad Street OX1 3AJ | Getting there Bus 6 or 13; a 10-minute walk east from Oxford Station | Hours Accessible 24 hours | Tip Head west to George Gilbert Scott's 1843 Martyrs' Memorial shaped in the form of an Eleanor Cross on Magdalen Street.

65 Mesopotamia Whirlpool
The vortex between the rivers

No, it's not the land between the Tigris and the Euphrates in Babylonia (okay, Iraq). Mesopotamia, as any good Classics scholar knows, means 'between the rivers'. Because Oxford majors in smart alec antiquated esoterica, there just had to be a local enclave that featured the name. It has certainly been well chosen. Head east of the science sector to a path known as Mesopotamia Walk, with signs helpfully warning that it is for cyclists only – no pedestrians. Continue east where you will be confounded by a host of tributaries of the River Cherwell and associated streams. And eventually there it is: the Mesopotamia Whirlpool.

It is ferocious. It is fierce. It is fearsome. It may be related to Homer's Charybdis, a deadly eddy that would sink ships. It may be the brother of Edgar Allan Poe's Maelström, in the centre of which is an abyss penetrating the globe, and in which a bear, 'attempting to swim across the water, was caught by the stream and borne down, while he roared terribly, so as to be heard on shore'. More prosaically, Mesopotamia is a scenic river island nestled between the Cherwell's lower and upper levels.

To the north, there used to be an open-air bathing area known as Parson's Pleasure. This was a private place for male-only clothes-less body-washing. Women were forbidden, and a path diverted them away from it on punting trips. On one wonderful occasion a ladies' punt drifted past, to the embarrassment of a number of Oxford dons bathing in the altogether. They were quick to protect their modesty; however, the Warden of Wadham College covered not his genitals but his face, explaining 'I don't know about you, gentlemen, but in Oxford, *I*, at least, am known by my face!'. Unfortunately, the town spoilsports have closed it down. They've even got rid of the women-only version, 'Dame's Delight'. There's nothing stopping you taking an unofficial plunge though.

Address Mesopotamia Walk OX1 3TN | **Getting there** It's some distance from any public transport. By car, head north from High Street along Longwall Street and then take St Cross Road. At the junction with South Parks Road, Mesopotamia Walk goes off to the east. | **Hours** Accessible 24 hours | **Tip** To the south is Addison's Walk, originally Water Walk, a most picturesque footpath in the grounds of Magdalen College, named after Joseph Addison, co-founder of the *Spectator*, Britain's greatest magazine.

66 Most Famous Cross

Captured in much-loved famous nursery rhyme

No other market town has a cross so well known, and that's thanks to the famous nursery rhyme that starts 'Ride a cock horse to Banbury Cross / To see a fine lady upon a white horse'. But who was the 'fine lady'? Was it the naturist Lady Godiva herself, 11th-century Countess of Mercia, or Queen Elizabeth, who once visited? However, the cross from the lyrics is not the one that stands in the centre of the town, but the long-gone 20-foot High Cross that stood inside Market Square, where preachers would rant.

That cross met a terrible end at the hand of the Puritans, who declared it to be pagan. At dawn on 26 July, 1600, two masons started to pull it down, incensed at the carvings of Christ upon the Cross and the Madonna with child, and they were soon joined by a huge crowd only too keen to help. Once it was fallen, the bailiff, Henry Shewell, cried: 'God be thanked, Dagon, the deluder of the people, is fallen down'. Presumably the locals knew that Dagon was a Philistine priest from Biblical times in whose temple he and his tribe had hidden the Hebrews' Ark of the Covenant. In a move that Indiana Jones would have approved of, the morning after the seizing of the Ark, the statue of Dagon was found crumbled next to the stolen relic.

Banbury is a town of crosses. There was the 1441 Bread Cross at the corner of High Street and Butchers Row. It was covered, featured a slate roof to keep the butchers and bakers dry, and was where the poor would generously be given bread every Good Friday. It and the White Cross were pulled down in 1600. The 52-foot cross you can now see went up in 1859 to commemorate the wedding of Princess Vicky to the eventual Frederick III of Prussia, the 99-days emperor. The cross contains statues of Queen Victoria, Edward VII and George V, along with the town's motto *Dominus nobis sol et scutum* – 'The Lord is our sun and shield'.

Address Junction of Banbury High Street and Horse Fair | Getting there The cross is at the junction of the A 361 and the B 4035, right in the middle of the town; a 20-minute walk from Banbury Station | Hours Accessible 24 hours | Tip After examining the Cross in detail, head a short distance east to the Banbury Cross Inn.

67 Most Famous Debating Soc

Setting for the world's greatest arguments

Some of Britain's greatest politicians – Edwina Currie, Jacob Rees-Mogg, Ann Widdecombe, Boris – cut their oratorical skills as officers of what is one of the world's leading debating forums: the Oxford Union. The institution was founded in 1823 and is housed in a building near Carfax mostly designed by Alfred Waterhouse (Natural History Museum, Strangeways Prison), whose glorious Old Library contains murals painted by Pre-Raphaelite greats William Morris and Dante Gabriel Rossetti.

The Oxford Union hits the headlines when controversial motions are put forward or invitations cancelled because the speaker is a complete shower. In 1933, the infamous King and Country debate saw the room agree 'This House would under no circumstances fight for its King and Country'. Britain was horrified. The *Daily Telegraph* raged 'Disloyalty at Oxford. Gesture towards the Reds'. Randolph Churchill, son of Winston, tried to wipe the motion from the Union's minute book, which led to the interesting spectacle of Churchill being chased around Oxford by undergraduates wanting to debag him – remove his trousers without his consent. Wind on a few years and they're off to fight the Nazis anyway.

Some speakers never make it. In 1998 the Oxford Union invited Britain's leading fascist, the National Front's John Tyndall. The cops said no, citing a series of racially motivated attacks in London. Three years later, the Holocaust denier, David Irving, never made it. But that didn't stop a 2007 invitation to try once again, not just for Irving but the latest fascist of the day, Nick Griffin – both of them – on the topic of free speech. Cue mass protest, with guests prevented from entering and a sit-in in the debating chamber. Marine le Pen of France's National Front did, however, get past the blockaders to speak in 2015.

Address Frewin Court OX1 3JB, +44 (0)1865 241353, www.oxford-union.org | Getting there Bus 6 or 13; Oxford Station is nearby | Hours The Union welcomes visitors to the Old Library to view the murals: term time Mon–Fri 9.30am–7pm, Sat 11am–5pm; out of term Mon–Fri 9.30am–5pm | Tip Have some more heated rows at the nearby Wig and Pen hostelry.

68__Most Wonderful Street
High on the High

Visitors, poets, writers and wordsmiths from every corner of Britain, nay the world, have long waxed lyrical about High Street. For it is a main street without compare: grand, glorious, graceful; busy, booming, beautiful. Writing in 1974, Nikolaus Pevsner, the leading architectural critic, claimed that 'the High Street is one of the world's great streets. It has everything'. Long before, in 1820, the poet William Wordsworth noted 'the stream-like windings of that glorious street'. Eighteen years later, the German art historian Gustave Friedrich Waagen explained how 'the High Street of Oxford has not its equal in the whole world'. In 1895, Thomas Hardy has a carter stating in his novel *Jude the Obscure*: 'And there's a street in the place – the main street – that ha'n't another like it in the world'.

High Street stretches east from Carfax with slight, graceful turns towards Magdalen Bridge. It is at the centre of city life. Here are tasty cafés, exclusive shops, the posh boys' tailor Ede & Ravenscroft and buildings laced with history. At the western end, near Carfax, the substantial Covered Market is one of the best of its kind in the country: quality goods rather than cast-offs. At the eastern end is the glorious Botanic Garden. In between, two magnificent churches, the grandiose Grand Café, historical quirks such as William Morris' first shop, and most importantly a host of colleges – All Souls, Brasenose, Magdalen, Oriel, Queen's, St Edmund Hall and University College. When tourists ask: 'Exactly where is the university?', this is where you take them. It starts here.

There's even the chance of bumping into a rabid, raucous, radical row of remonstrators under the Cecil Rhodes statue. The only thing missing now is a decent pub. The historic Mitre closed in 2019 so that Lincoln College could turn it into student accommodation, but it later reopened as a restaurant.

Address High Street OX1 4AH | **Getting there** Bus 3, 3A, 8 or 10; the western end is a 12-minute walk from Oxford Station | **Hours** Accessible 24 hours | **Tip** To maximise the High Street experience, explore the enticing side streets that veer off north and south.

69 Muses Atop the Clarendon
Check the roof for inspiration

With the Clarendon Building of 1711, Nicholas Hawksmoor (1661–1736), Christopher Wren's most celebrated pupil and among Britain's greatest ever architects, created an imposing grand portico to what was to be an even grander entrance to Oxford University – literally a gateway to learning. So it's only fitting that this landmark Oxford structure is topped with nine statues representing the Muses. They were created by Sir James Thornhill and cost £600, yet the University initially turned them down and they lay in storage for two years before finally being erected. Seven originals remain, but Euterpe and Melpomene later fell down and were replaced in 1974 with fibreglass copies given by Blackwell's bookshop across the road.

The Clarendon was originally the Printing House, built to store the Oxford University Press. When the OUP moved to new premises in Walton Street, Jericho, in the 1820s, the building became the Clarendon, the name chosen because it was partly paid for by the profits from Lord Clarendon's *History of the Great Rebellion.* The police then took over part of the building, mostly to house the local toms, and the rest of the Clarendon came to be used by the university for admin. The Clarendon was later taken over by the Bodleian Library, and now houses the Clarendon Fund, a major graduate scholarship scheme that offers around 140 new scholarships every year on the basis of academic excellence across all degree-bearing subjects.

In January 2009 demonstrators occupied part of the building to condemn Israel and cancel a lecture series to be given at nearby Balliol by the country's president, Shimon Peres. They called on Oxford University to 'release a statement in support of the rights of Palestinians'. Or, as a Christ Church student noted: 'The students don't want to solve anything, but just want to feel good and self-righteous about a cause.'

Address 48 Broad Street OX1 3AZ, +44 (0)1865 277000 | **Getting there** Bus 6 or 13; a 10-minute walk east from Oxford Station | **Hours** Accessible 24 hours | **Tip** A must to visit, immediately south, is the Bodleian Library, Britain's second largest, established in 1602 and containing over 11 million works (visit.bodleian.ox.ac.uk).

70 __ Narnia Door
Portal to a magical world

One minute you're walking down St Mary's Passage between Brasenose and All Souls; the next you've gone through a portal into Narnia,
a fantasy world of magic, mythical beasts and talking animals. Well,
maybe just in your imagination, for half way down this romantic and
atmospheric passage is a magnificent, ornate, olde-worlde door that
inspired C. S. Lewis' flights of fancy.

The door features a gold fauns on either side that resemble
Mr Tumnus from *The Lion, The Witch and the Wardrobe*, while wooden
carvings on the front look like the lion Aslan who protects Narnia
from evil. A little further along is an old oil lamp post that could be
the notable landmark post in Narnia. In *The Chronicles of Narnia* series
(1950–56), Lucy Pevensie is the first of the four Pevensie children
to find the wardrobe entrance to Narnia: 'It will not go out of my
mind that if we pass this post and lantern, either we shall find strange
adventures or else some great changes of our fortunes'.

C. S. Lewis, the Oxford don responsible for the seven Narnia
fantasy novels, was born in Belfast, and studied Classics and English Literature at Oxford's University College. He took a First in
Mods and Greats, and was appointed a tutor in philosophy. Oxford
proved a fertile breeding ground for his ideas, drawing on centuries-old buildings, mesmerising monuments, and cobbled streets to
create his extraordinary world of fantasy.

He also imbued these popular works with much Christian symbolism. His closest friend was an even more celebrated fantasy novelist – J. R. R. Tolkien – and the pair led a group of like-minded
intellectuals known as The Inklings. Tolkien had a huge influence
over Lewis, especially regarding themes of redemption and religion,
and the two could often be seen huddling over Christian texts or
Middle Earth manuscripts in the local pubs such as The Eagle and
Child (see ch. 51).

Address St Mary's Passage, OX1 3BW | Getting there Bus 3, 3A, 6 or 8; the area is a 10 to 15 minute walk east from Oxford Station | **Hours** Outside accessible 24 hours | **Tip** For another magical portal experience, take the short walk to look for Christopher Wren's 'Doorway to God', a divine entrance to the Sheldonian Theatre, decorated with the university coat of arms.

71 Not so Cool for Catz

Modernist torment from a great Dane

Quadrangles and towers dripping in 15th-century honey-coloured stone? Cloisters, cobbles, corbels and keystones with Classical decorations? Not at St Catherine's, where Danish architect Arne Jacobsen created a campus with an egalitarian theme using glass, brick and concrete.

The college is a youngster in Oxford terms, for it was founded as recently as 1962 when the St Catherine's Society was given full college status thanks to historian Alan Bullock who raised a million from a businessman he met by chance on RMS *Queen Mary*. And so with a typical burst of 1960s experimentation, Jacobsen was hired to design everything – furniture, cutlery, lampshades and chairs. The buildings even have a Grade I listing. The only problem is – they're vile. They belong in Ordsall, not Oxford. No matter how progressive and futurist, they are hideous to look at: rectangular, linear, boxy. They recall the prefabs of the 1950s. They reek of the disastrous town planning precinct mistakes of the 1960s. You know the college is pushing it when their website talks of Jacobsen's 'challenge of creating an integrated environment which would be both practical and aesthetically pleasing…'. Come on fellas, this is waffle. Folk come to Oxford for secluded cloisters and romantic, ivy-covered Cotswold stone, not for a glass Lego set. Yet St Catherine's was one of the first to admit women, in 1974.

When Jacobsen visited the city, he noticed that the students' gowns were often in tatters. They told him it was because they had to climb over the college walls when they came back late and that the gowns were useful for covering the protruding glass shards. The great Dane died in 1971, but he would have loved a recent Covid-era row when some students, wait for it, 'coughed at staff'. According to journalists, the college 'blasted the reprehensible individuals'. All seems so quaint now.

Address Manor Road OX1 3UJ, +44 (0)1865 271700, www.stcatz.ox.ac.uk | Getting there Bus 280 or ST1; a 30-minute walk from Oxford Station | Hours Daily 9am–5pm | Tip Head east to Marston Road to gaze in awe at the Islamic Studies Centre, which has graduated from a wooden hut on St Cross Road to this magnificent baroque palace.

72 __ The Office
'Customers with the highest IQ in the world'

The King's Arms pub, owned by Wadham College and first licensed in 1607, is the oldest ale house in its original position in Oxford. It was so named as taverns at that time wanted to show allegiance to the new king of Britain, James I, who had been James VI of Scotland when he left Edinburgh.

The first local performance of *Hamlet* took place here soon after, but more regular entertainments were fights with swords and singlesticks. For centuries, the King's Arms was also a major stop for students and other intellectuals discussing the most important subjects in the universe. Regulars joked that its customers had 'the highest IQ in the world'. In 1944 the novelist Graham Greene could be seen drinking here with Kim Philby, later the intelligence officer and communist double agent who defected to the Soviets. Warren Lewis, brother of the Narnia writer C. S. Lewis, came here in May 1945 to drown his sorrows on the death of fellow Inklings member, the poet Charles Williams. He wrote in his diary: 'I feel dazed and restless, and went out to get a drink, choosing unfortunately the King's Arms. There will be no more pints with Charles; the blackout has fallen, and the Inklings can never be the same'.

In the 1960s, dons held tutorials in the back bar, earning the pub the nickname 'The Office'. Around that time a drinkers' horror story unfolded: the brewery insisted that the pub serve the undrinkable Double Diamond, a keg concoction. The pub's back room, the 'Dons' Bar', wasn't open to women until 1973, the year when a fire, rumoured to have been started by radical feminists, broke out. Even as recently as the late 20th century, women entering on their own were frowned at. Members of the anti-social toffs' club, the Bullingdon, were barred in 2006 after they started a fire and smashed an antique mirror. A recent ban on outside drinking has now fortunately been lifted.

Address 40 Holywell Street, Oxford OX1 3SP, +44 (0)1865 242369, www.kingsarmsoxford.co.uk | Getting there Bus 3, 3A, 8 or 10; a 20-minute walk from Oxford Station | Hours Daily 11am–11pm | Tip Soak up the alcohol a few doors east at the Tuck Shop or even a little further east at the Alternative Tuck Shop.

73 Peace Stone
Napoleon surrendering in a roundabout way

You're unlikely to see Napoleon's ferocious forces storming their way into Oxford along the A 420, and just to prove it, here on the Plain, the roundabout at the eastern end of High Street, is the Peace Stone.

This memorial honours the Treaty of Paris, signed on 30 May, 1814 to bring about the *pax Europa*. Peace followed a month later when Napoleon was imprisoned on Elba, and two peace stones went up in Oxford to commemorate the event. A thanksgiving day took place on 7 July as the Mayor of Oxford, Joseph Lock, explained that it would 'concert measures for gladdening the hearts of the Poor of Oxford'. The proclamation was greeted with loud cheers, and barrels of strong beer were stationed around town amidst much excitement. Remarkably, wars kept on breaking out, and so in April 1856, another Proclamation of Peace had to be made, this time to mark the end of the Crimean War. Announcements took place all over Oxford – at Carfax, St Mary's and at all four gates.

This land was then occupied by St Clement's Church that stood just outside the city boundaries in Bruggeset. The church was demolished in 1829 as it was considered too small. According to reports 'services were very much interrupted and annoyed by the continued noise of carriages passing to and fro'. And this despite the fact that one of the greatest figures of 19th-century Christianity, John Henry Newman, originally an Anglican priest, later a Catholic cardinal, canonised in 2019, was curate there for two years in the 1820s.

The demolition of St Clement left a wide expanse that was given the name The Plain. Long gone, too, is the tollbooth for the turnpike here at the start of the road to London via Henley, as is a war memorial dedicated to the 142 men of the First Battalion Oxfordshire Light Infantry who died in the Second Boer War (1899 – 1902) and which now stands outside the barracks in Abingdon.

74 Penrose Paving
Do the math

A tiling pattern in the pavement outside Oxford's Andrew Wiles building is named after Roger Penrose, the famous mathematician who devised the design in the 1970s. The paving is created from two different diamond-shaped granite tiles, each embellished with circular stainless steel arcs. The shape is of kites and darts, and the pattern is aperiodic. In other words, it is not possible to create the tiling by taking a section and repeating it over and over again. The paving was unveiled in 2013 and now has a geometric cousin in a street in Helsinki.

For those of a higher level mathematical bent, the pattern has an 'inflation property which proves the non-periodicity of any such tiling. If some region could be repeated over and over again to yield the whole tiling, this same region would have to be a period parallelogram for the inflated darts and kites too'. For those not of a mathematical bent, it's a nice bit of crazy paving.

Roger Penrose, born 1931, is Britain's leading mathematician and an expert in cosmology. He has long bucked establishment points of view, contradicting his elders with new facts such as claiming that the universe didn't start with the Big Bang. Penrose shared the 1988 Wolf Prize for Physics with Stephen Hawking, and the 2020 Nobel Prize in Physics after discovering that black holes can predict Einstein's general theory of relativity. The committee explained how 'the discoveries of this year's laureates have broken new ground in the study of compact and supermassive objects'. In his thousand-page tome *The Road to Reality*, his masterpiece, Penrose gives an overview of the whole of physics as it stands today.

But if you do bump into him knocking back a swift half in the nearby Jude the Obscure pub, never mind e=mc^2, just get him to explain how 1+2+3+4 all the way up to infinity equals negative 1 divided by 12. Yes, really!

Address Andrew Wiles Building, 43 Woodstock Road OX2 6GG | **Getting there** Bus 6 or S6; a 20-minute walk from Oxford Station | **Hours** Accessible 24 hours | **Tip** Marvel in awe at the Classical temple that is the nearby Radcliffe Observatory. It was designed in 1794 by James Wyatt of the famous family of architects, who based the tower on Athens' Tower of Winds.

75 Queen Matilda's Castle
The Great Escape

Forget Mary Tudor. Matilda (c. 1102–67), should have been the first sole queen of England. In 1135 Henry I named her, his daughter, as his successor, to be the first ever English queen to rule in her own right after his son, William Adelin, drowned when his ship sank in the Channel. Unfortunately, her cousin Stephen thought otherwise. He led a coup and raced to Winchester to be crowned first, so Matilda hot-footed it to Oxford and based her campaign at the castle. Cue: civil war, battles, sieges, captures, a conflict known as the Anarchy.

When King Stephen was captured and imprisoned, Matilda briefly ruled as the 'Lady of the English'. Coins were issued with her face, and a date was announced for her coronation. But it wasn't to be. In 1142 Stephen besieged Oxford Castle, only to find the fortress impregnable, and this, St George's Tower, too high to overcome. After three months, Matilda, dressed in a white cloak and using ropes, escaped from the tower on a cold snowy December night. She fled across the frozen Isis (Oxfordspeak for the Thames) and reached safety at Abingdon, six miles away. The Anarchy continued for 10 more years, with neither side the winner, but eventually a compromise was reached: Stephen would remain on the throne, after which Matilda's son would become King Henry II of England.

Oxford Castle was built by Robert d'Oilly in the 1070s after William the Conqueror had granted him substantial estates. Oxford was considered to be of strategic importance due to its location on the Thames. A surprisingly large section of the castle remains, and has been refurbished for tourism. Visitors can climb the Saxon St George's Tower, the mound of the 11th-century motte-and-bailey section, or descend underground into the 900-year-old crypt to see the remains of St George's Chapel where Geoffrey of Monmouth penned the Legends of King Arthur.

Address 44–46 Oxford Castle OX1 1AY, +44 (0)1865 260663, www.oxfordcastleandprison.co.uk | **Getting there** Bus 4A; Oxford Station is nearby | **Hours** Daily 10am–5pm | **Tip** Part of the surrounding five-acre site is occupied by the boutique Malmaison Hotel. It's a bit unusual; it used to be the prison (www.malmaison.com).

76 Queen of Colleges

'The grandest Classical architecture in Oxford'

Queen's is the queen of colleges because, amongst its many qualities, the main buildings were designed by Britain's two greatest ever architects, Christopher Wren and Nicholas Hawksmoor, whose designs were completed in the 18th century and described by Pevsner as 'the grandest piece of Classical architecture in Oxford'.

The college was founded in 1341 as the Hall of the Queen's Scholars of Oxford by Robert de Eglesfield. The queen was Philippa of Hainault, wife of Edward III, king of England. Initially membership was aimed at chaplains, poor boys and servants. Though the college started poor, its assets improved through owning land in Southampton and the growth of their docks. In 2018, the college was gifted £290 million, making it one of the wealthiest.

Famous alumni include the pioneering philosopher Jeremy Bentham (1760–63), who explained that 'it is the greatest happiness of the greatest number that is the measure of right and wrong'. Bentham pioneered the idea of women's suffrage. His preserved skeleton is kept on public display at the main entrance of University College, London. Edmond Halley (1763–66) was the second Astronomer Royal and helped fund the publication of Isaac Newton's *Principia Mathematica* (1687). He gave his name to the most famous comet, which he predicted to return in 1758, but which he did not live to see. While studying physics at Queen's, Tim Berners-Lee (1973–76), who went on to invent the World Wide Web, made a computer out of an old television set, which he bought from a repair shop. He launched the first web site, which described what it was and what he had done, on 20 December, 1990. Rowan Atkinson (1975), the future hapless Mr Bean, arrived to do a Masters in Electrical Engineering. He made his name with *Not the Nine O'Clock News* and then took the lead role of Edmund Blackadder in the historical spoof of the same name.

Address High Street, immediately west of Queen's Lane OX1 4AW, +44 (0)1865 279120, www.queens.ox.ac.uk | **Getting there** Bus 3, 3A, 8 or 10; the western end is a 12-minute walk from Oxford Station | **Hours** The College is not open to members of the public, although it is possible to visit the Chapel for services and concerts | **Tip** Just east is the rather more obscure St Edmund Hall (known as Teddy Hall), which claims to be the oldest surviving academic society in the world (www.seh.ox.ac.uk).

77 RAF Brize Norton
Airport fit for princes

Brize Norton is the country's chief military airport. It's where troops leave to go and fight. Indeed, it was from Brize Norton that the country's two favourite princes, Andrew and Harry, left and returned many times over the years to keep the British flag flying high in strategic outposts such as the Falklands and Afghanistan. It's also where Andrew did his training in how to use a helicopter and how not to sweat. Yet when Harry, sorry Second Lieutenant Wales, returned to Britain here in 2008 critics cried 'publicity stunt'. As if.

The airport is also used for transporting nuclear weapons full of plutonium and enriched uranium. If that sounds worrying, the public can be reassured to discover that an MoD emergency exercise monitors what might happen if two such nuclear-carrying planes were to crash into each other. But Brize Norton also witnesses tragic events. In March 2003, the bodies of British servicemen who had died in Iraq were brought back as the band played Handel's 'Dead March'. In January 2017 there was a disturbing incident when a group of anti-deportation activists were rounded up and put on a secret expulsion flight from here. It followed a nasty episode at Stansted where they had chained themselves to the wheels of a jet bound for West Africa.

Occasionally, there's a bit of surreal drama. In October 2019 a film crew shooting the latest James Bond picture accidentally left a van behind. When staff spotted it, they went into full anti-terrorism mode and evacuated 400 personnel. What a disappointment when it was only found to contain some stale M&S sandwiches the crew couldn't stomach. In February 2022, typhoon jets were scrambled because four Russian military aircraft were approaching the UK. Were they bringing Vladimir Putin for one of his regular trips to the nearest McDonald's, given the poor quality of Big Macs in Moscow? It was never disclosed.

Address Carterton OX18 3LX | Getting there By air or by road on the B 4477 |
Hours Accessible 24 hours | Tip Sup where the pilots sup in the Swan Inn or
Maytime Inn to the north.

78 Randolph Hotel
Temporary home to the stars

King Alfonso of Spain, Farouk of Egypt, the Clintons, Mikhail Gorbachev, Alec Guinness… that's just a short list of the rich, famous and really important who have stayed at Oxford's very grandest hotel. The Randolph is *the* place for students to impress their parents, courtesy of the afternoon tea, for which a second and third mortgage might be a necessity, although no one can complain about the quality of the fayre or how they manage to cut the sandwiches into perfect isosceles triangles.

The hotel was built in the 1860s following a debate about whether the building should be Classical or Gothic, the latter winning, which is why it resembles the Oxford University Museum. Gullible tourists, hoping to soak up stories of traditional England, are told not that the hotel is named in honour of a Dr Francis Randolph, an 18th-century university benefactor, but after Lord Randolph Churchill, father of Winston. And it was the 21-year-old Churchill père who was summoned before the university beak in March 1870 after exiting the hotel having clearly downed too much juice and seizing a constable, 'pushing and shoving him and taking hold of his cape'. To add insult to injury, the good lord then offered the copper five pounds. Churchill and his pals made off down the street with the unfortunate officer in hot pursuit.

One day in the 1920s, the *Brideshead Revisited* novelist Evelyn Waugh shocked diners at the Randolph by interrupting a discussion on bisexuality and declaring 'Buggers can have babies'. Kingsley Amis' future wife Hilly used to sneak into the hotel to wash her hair and underwear, while she was staying with him. Disaster struck in 2015 when a nasty fire broke out, possibly caused by the flambéed beef. At least there were no casualties, apart from the beef. The Randolph has featured in many Morse episodes and there is a Morse Bar.

Address Beaumont Street OX1 2LN, +44 (0)344 8799132, www.graduatehotels.com/
oxford-uk | Getting there Bus 6 or 13; Oxford Station is nearby | Tip Next door is the
Oxford Playhouse where many greats have trodden the boards, including Richard Burton
and Elizabeth Taylor in *Doctor Faustus* in 1966 (www.oxfordplayhouse.com).

79 Rhodes Hasn't Fallen
Diamonds might not be forever

Cecil Rhodes was one of the most zealous promoters of the British Empire – hell, they even named Rhodesia in east Africa after him. He founded the De Beers diamond corporation, the most successful the world has ever seen, and infamously said 'to be born English is to win first prize in the lottery of life'. Yet today, hordes of activists demand that Cecil Rhodes' barely noticeable statue high above the door of Oriel College on High Street should be torn down.

To complicate matters, Rhodes in his will established the Rhodes Scholarship. Every year, around 100 international students study at Oxford under the scheme, one of the most prestigious in the world. Past beneficiaries include Bill Clinton and Kris Kristofferson. The campaign to topple his statue began in earnest in 2015. A year later, students at the Oxford Union debating society voted 245 to 212 in favour of removing it.

However, the university announced that the statue would remain after 'furious donors' threatened to withdraw gifts and bequests worth more than £100 million. The campaign flared up again in June 2020 in the wake of the murder of George Floyd in America, which led to campaigns to bring down those now considered to be on the wrong side of history.

In May 2021, sculptor Antony Gormley came up with an ingenious alternative – turning the statue around so that it faced the wall. Instead, the university put up a plaque, explaining that Rhodes 'obtained his fortune through exploitation of minerals, land and peoples of southern Africa'. Cue protest from more reasoned academics citing lack of balance. David Abulafia, emeritus professor of Mediterranean history at Cambridge, noted that 'Rhodes believed he was bringing benefits to Africa. We might now argue that he did more harm than good but one has to understand what his intentions were. He is portrayed here as some sort of devil incarnate'.

Address Outside Oriel College OX1 4EW, www.oriel.ox.ac.uk | **Getting there** Bus 3, 3A, 8 or 10; the western end is a 12-minute walk from Oxford Station | **Hours** Accessible 24 hours | **Tip** After gazing at the dodgy statue for hours, you might need some sustenance at nearby Rick's Diner, no relation to Suzanne Vega's Tom's Diner.

80_ The Roundheads' Pub

No earthly reason not to visit

The acclaimed 14th-century Turf Tavern is tucked away off a tiny alley by Holywell Street. It was deliberately built on a dry moat just outside the city walls to avoid the jurisdiction of the local colleges' governing bodies. Indeed, a remaining section of the old city wall runs along one side of the building.

Fittingly, the Turf and its environs have a history worthy of the most bibulous of backgrounds. During medieval plagues, cats were set alight and thrown over the city wall here in a failed attempt to transfer the disease to the beasts. The Roundheads supporting Oliver Cromwell during the English Civil War of the 1640s would meet here to discuss how to put an end to the monarchy, even though Oxford was a royalist stronghold. The pub was long a haven for illegal gambling, and fittingly earned a mention in Thomas Hardy's *Jude the Obscure* (1895) as a 'low-ceilinged tavern up a court', where Jude courts Arabella in the company of 'a red-faced auctioneer, two stone masons, some horsey men in the know of betting circles…'.

The pub's most remarkable claim to fame is that it was here in 1954 that future Australian Prime Minister Bob Hawke set a Guinness world record for downing a yard of ale in 11 seconds. Maybe Hawke supped too much, because he later claimed that the record was set not at the Turf but at the nearby dining hall of University College where he was a student, as punishment for failing to wear his academic gown to dinner. 'Some bastard had borrowed mine, so I was sconced' – forced to drink from a pewter pot or face a fine. 'I downed the contents of the pot in 11 seconds, left the sconcemaster floundering. This feat was to endear me to some of my fellow Australians more than anything else I ever achieved.' Later, more famous, drinkers who have not been in such a hurry include Margaret Thatcher, Bill Clinton and Stephen Hawking.

Address 4 Bath Place OX1 3SU, +44 (0)1865 243235, www.theturftavern.co.uk |
Getting there Bus 3, 3A, 8 or 10; a 20-minute walk from Oxford Station | **Hours** Daily
11am – 11pm | **Tip** Take a little trip east to St Cross Church, now a historic collections
centre for Balliol College.

81 Ruins of Osney Abbey
Is that all there is?

The house of Augustinian canons by the Thames has long gone. So have the canons. So intense has been its demise that all that's left is this forlorn-looking 15th-century stone arch and bit of wall on Mill Street. There is a plaque, but it might as well be quoting the words of one of Oxford University's greatest poets – Shelley – 'Look on my works ye mighty and despair'.

Osney Abbey was founded in 1129. Its monks were ingenious engineers, even moving the River Thames several hundred yards. In 1222, the Archbishop of Canterbury held a special all-England church council here, which ruled that St George's Day, 23 April, was to be a holiday and George, not St Edmund the Martyr, England's patron saint. It also declared that Jews should not mix with Christians and had to wear a special badge. When the papal legate came to stay in 1237, local students planned to ply him with copious amounts of roast meats and strong wine, plus the inevitable working girl. The Vatican man was kosher, so it didn't come off. Nevertheless, a group of student heavies marched on the abbey, only to be repelled by security, resulting in a farcical state of affairs with the Italian delegation hurling Latin insults at the failed invaders. Not to be put off, the student army collected tree trunks as a battering ram, attacked again, and were now met with boiling oil poured from above. Eventually, King John's army stormed to Oxford to sort out the chaos, and 38 students were rounded up.

The abbey was dissolved in 1539 and converted into a cathedral. Many artefacts were given to nearby Christ Church, including what is now Tom Tower bell. But Osney faded away and the stone was plundered. Many local historians believe it to be the greatest building that Oxford has lost. Their mill survived for centuries, but was gutted by fire in 1945 and its outer walls incorporated into a block of flats.

Address Mill Street OX2 0AJ | Getting there Bus 33, 400 or 423; a short walk from Oxford Station | Hours Accessible 24 hours | Tip Head to the Thames and make southwards for a glorious constitutional to Grandpont.

82 Sheldonian Emperor Heads

Trying not to lose theirs

The railings of this Christopher Wren building, where the annual degree-awarding ceremonies take place, feature 17 fascinating stone heads known popularly as the Oxford Emperors. These are the third set. Originally there were 14, carved in 1669 in Clipsham stone by William Byrd as part of Wren's overall design and modelled on the sages of antiquity, not the 12 Caesars as some have alleged. Their faces suggested shock and surprise, which many said reflected the minimal budget Gilbert Sheldon, Archbishop of Canterbury, had offered Wren. Over the years the heads suffered the ravages of time.

The Victorians replaced them but used the wrong kind of stone and the new heads became farcical misshapen lumps. Nevertheless, Max Beerbohm heaped praise on the heads in his 1911 novel *Zuleika Dobson*: 'Here in Oxford, exposed eternally and inexorably to wind and frost, to the four winds that lash them and the rains that wear them away, they are expiating, in effigy, the abominations of their pride and cruelty and lust'. But John Betjeman noted their decay and derided them as 'the mouldering busts round the Sheldonian' in his 1960 autobiography *Summoned by Bells*.

Fortunately, a new set arrived in 1972 courtesy of sculptor Michael Black who went to the extraordinary lengths of searching for the originals in the gardens of Oxford. He located five and later another two that had somehow migrated to Herefordshire. Black modelled his new heads on Wren's to capture the same looks of shock and surprise. Each displays a different type of beard.

When the Dalai Lama gave a talk at the Sheldonian in May 2008 he was met by protesters from the Chinese Western Shugden Society who filled Broad Street with chants of 'Dalai Lama stop lying', accusing Lhamo Thondup of banning traditional Buddhist prayer and abusing the human rights of Shugden Buddhists.

Address Broad Street OX1 3AZ | Getting there Bus 6 or 13; a 10-minute walk east from Oxford Station | Hours Accessible 24 hours | Tip More cultural antiquity required? No trip to Oxford is complete without a visit to the world famous Ashmolean Museum on Beaumont Street (www.ashmolean.org).

83 Sodom Wadham

Remember Lot's wife

What on earth has Wadham College done to deserve such a nickname? It can't just be the statue of James I over the Front Quad. It might be because one of its most infamous alumni is John Wilmot, second earl of Rochester (1647–80), whose poem, 'The Debauchee', summed up his loose, licentious lifestyle: 'I rise at Eleven, I dine about Two / I get drunk before Sev'n; and the next Thing I do / I send for my whore, when for fear of the Clap…'. He died from VD at 33. Johnny Depp played him in the 2004 film *The Libertine.*

Robert Thistlethwayte, 18th-century Warden, was caught trying to seduce Master William French, 'a commoner of the College'. The particulars were judged 'too gross and obscene to be repeated', so Thistlethwayte had to flee to France. And let's not forget Maurice Bowra, Warden 1938–70, brilliant wit, who once quipped that: 'Buggery was invented to fill that awkward hour between evensong and cocktails'.

Yet this is the college where the saintly priest John Wilkins, inventor of the metric system as a religious tribute to the Hebrews' 2,000 cubits, was Warden in the 1640s. Nowadays, Wadham is making its intake more diverse by looking at applications from schools such as Rugby or Westminster, rather than just Eton. Of those who don't get in, some deal with it more imaginatively than others. When 18-year-old Claudia Vulliamy was rejected in 2017, she did a bit of a William Burroughs with the letter, cut it up, and converted it into a celebrated work of Mondrianesque abstract art. A picture of the piece on social media was retweeted 48,000 times.

Anyone still thinking of applying to Wadham must beware Emeritus Fellow and arch communist Terry Eagleton who dismissed the collapse of the Soviet-styled regimes at the end of the 1980s as a 'mild irritant', and told one class that it was just as valid to deconstruct the telephone directory as it is to read Shakespeare.

Address Parks Road OX1 3PN, +44 (0)1865 277900, www.wadham.ox.ac.uk | **Getting there** Bus 3, 3A, 8 or 10; a 20-minute walk from Oxford Station | **Hours** Term time 1–4.15pm, out of term 10.30–11.45am & 1–4.15pm | **Tip** A few hundred yards north is Rhodes House, its stark Classical façade based on the Temple of Athena Polias at Priene, Turkey, and its name daringly honouring the infamous colonialist Cecil Rhodes.

84 St Frideswide's Door

Patron saint escapes… carved by Alice herself?

Samuel Sanders Teulon was a manic Victorian church builder, responsible for nearly 100 Gothic revival structures. St Frideswide's, from 1872, is not only dedicated to the seventh-century patron saint of Oxford, but features a gorgeous door carving said to have been designed by Alice (in Wonderland) herself. But there is still much debate as to whether this door in a corner of the nave, which depicts Frideswide escaping from King Algar of Mercia who wanted to marry her, really was created by Alice Liddell, Lewis Carroll's model for the magical Alice. Others cite two of Alice's sisters, Rhoda and Violet.

St Frideswide was a seventh-century princess and abbess who founded a monastery that was later incorporated into one of Oxford's greatest colleges, Christ Church. Lovers of religious architecture of a mathematical bent come from far and wide to marvel at the door's *vesica piscis* – the curved arch reaching up to a point, the second most important shape in Christian sacred geometry, its proportions governed by obscure mathematical properties alluded to in the New Testament.

Oxford has so many glorious churches, Nikolaus Pevsner, the great architectural historian who journeyed throughout the country tracking down everything that didn't move, must have been having a bad day when he derided St Frideswide's as 'violently high Victorian… an example of architectural ruthlessness'. The great man later apologised and explained that his survey was done too quickly. Frideswide's name means 'peace' (*frithes*) and 'strong' (*withe*). She's still big news in Oxford. Art works show her holding a shepherd's staff beside a fountain springing up, one of the legends associated with her. There's stained glass by the great Edward Burne-Jones in Christ Church Cathedral, a Frideswide Square by the Saïd Business School, and a popular choir, the Frideswide Voices.

Address Botley Road, just west of Bridge Street OX2 0BL, +44 (0)1865 242345, www.osneybenefice.org.uk | Getting there The church is one minute west of Oxford Station | Hours Only open during services – check the website for times | Tip The Holly Bush Inn at 106 Bridge Street was the setting for early Radiohead gigs, in one case in front of six people. Yes, that many (www.hollybushoxford.co.uk).

85   St Giles

Fair dos

The street of St Giles is one of the most fascinating in Oxford. One feature that captivates the *flâneur* is its extreme width, as well as the two legendary pubs of the Eagle and Child and the Lamb and Flag, and the reason for its unusual size is because of the historic St Giles fair that takes place here every September.

The fair dates back to 1625 when it was a parish festival to celebrate the feast of St Giles, one of the 14 holy helpers, patron saint of the disabled. The fair came with some popular traditions: anyone with a beershop was allowed to bring barrels of ale to sell, plus, even more bibulously, any St Giles householder could sell the sauce during the fair by hanging the bough of a tree over their front door. Even Queen Elizabeth paid a visit in 1567, watching from the windows of St John's College.

In the 19th century, the fair became so rowdy and licentious there were moves to close it down. A terrible incident occurred in 1843 when a horse became frightened by the noise, and ran through the crowd knocking down 20 people and killing the wife of the Master of the Bluecoat School. After that, no horses were allowed beyond 12 noon, the perfect solution for horses that could tell the time.

John Betjeman, the much-loved late-20th-century poet laureate, described the fair's liveliness in his 1938 work *An Oxford University Chest*. 'It is about the biggest fair in England, thick with freak shows, roundabouts, cake-walks, the whip, and the witching waves.' But that was nothing to the scandal in 2021 when Hebborn & Son's waltzer ride displayed a sign that read: 'All topless girls ride free'. The council contacted the Showmen's Guild of Great Britain and asked them to 'rectify this urgently'. Surely this can't be the same Oxford in which Bullingdon Club and Piers Gaveston Society revellers take depravity to limits not seen since the last days of Pompeii?

Address St Giles OX1 3LE | Getting there Bus 6 or 13; a 20-minute walk from Oxford
Station | Hours Accessible 24 hours; for details of the fair, check Oxford City Council
website www.oxford.gov.uk for dates and times | Tip Where the roads fork at 10 Woodstock
Road is the ancient church of St Giles, named after the 8th-century Greek-born patron
saint of the handicapped who lived on wild roots, herbs and deer milk.

86 St John's Gate Tower

Storing up for themselves riches on Earth

St John's College – Alma Mater to the *Shropshire Lad* poet A. E. House-man, the novelist Kingsley Amis and the warrior prime minister Tony Blair – was founded in 1555 to provide Roman Catholic clerics who would support Mary Tudor's opposition to the Protestant Reforma-tion. It's Oxford's wealthiest college, which is hardly surprising given that it owns a number of pubs, a major contributor to its £600 million assets, although in recent years, really clever students have discovered that the St John's of the past made money through, wait for it, slavery!

One of its ex-students, William Laud, Charles I's Archbishop of Canterbury in the 1630s, was executed during the English Civil War after being accused of popery, tyranny and treason. However, he's had the last laugh, for his ghost haunts the college library that he helped build, and students who swear they've not been supping at the nearby college pub, the Lamb and Flag (see ch. 52), have claimed they've seen the spectral decapitated bish kicking his own head along the aisles.

St John's greatest alumnus is Philip Larkin, the finest English poet of the 20th century. He joined in October 1940, only because his appalling eyesight meant he was not fit to fight in the war. Here he met Kingsley Amis and they quickly hit it off through a mutual love of irreverence and ridicule. Colleagues and friends were surprised Larkin didn't take up an academic post but became a librarian. However, an unpublished letter recently discovered in a college safe revealed that his revulsion of literary parties – 'hell on earth… a lot of sherry-drill with important people', put him off becoming professor of poetry. Typ-ically, Larkin explained his antipathy magnificently in barbed verse:

'I could spend half my evenings, if I wanted/ Holding a glass of washing sherry, canted

Over to catch the drivel of some bitch / Who's read nothing but *Which*.'

Address St Giles OX1 3JP, +44 (0)1865 277300, www.sjc.ox.ac.uk | Getting there Bus 6 or 13; a 20-minute walk from Oxford Station | Hours Daily 1–5pm, or until dusk in the winter | Tip Head west to 16 St John Street and a blue plaque to discover the painter William Turner of Oxford, so named to distinguish him from the other Turner.

87 St Margaret's Well
Heal the sick, cast out demons

In the Mad Hatter's Tea Party in *Alice's Adventures in Wonderland*, the sleepy dormouse relates a nonsensical story of three little sisters who lived at the bottom of a treacle well. In case you think this came solely out of Lewis Carroll's wild, wonderful imagination, then visit Binsey's parish church, St Margaret of Antioch, with its holy well. To the medieval Oxonians, this really was a treacle well, because the very word 'treacle' came from the antiquated *theriac*, which referred to an ancient Greek panacea.

Pilgrims came from afar to be treated with the supposedly holy waters of what became known as St Margaret's Well, inspired by the legend of St Frideswide, the patron saint of Oxford. The Frideswide story has it that Algar of Mercia, a seventh-century prince, became infatuated with her and sought marriage. Bound by celibacy, Frideswide fled to Binsey in an attempt to escape her fate. This didn't put off Algar, but unfortunately, while searching Oxford for his bride-to-be, he was struck by lightning and blinded. Frideswide, being a kind and saintly saint, prayed to God, which brought forth a spring with healing waters. The prince was cured. He could now see!

Pilgrims over the years include Henry VIII and Catherine of Aragon. The royal couple sought its waters to help produce a royal son and heir. Imagine had the cure worked: the English Reformation might never have happened, Britain would still be Catholic, and there'd be no six wives of Henry VIII – just one wife.

The well was removed in 1639, but restored by the Revd T. J. Prout in 1874, thanks to Lewis Carroll. The church is filled with Gothic splendours: 12th-century lancet windows and stained glass depicting the martyrdom of Thomas Becket. After Frideswide died in October 727, her grave became a shrine for pilgrims. This was probably the first instance of Oxford as a tourist destination.

Address Binsey Lane OX2 0NG | **Getting there** Binsey Lane runs north from the A 420, just west of Oxford Station | **Hours** Accessible 24 hours | **Tip** A lifetime could be spent exploring the myriad of waterways that flow here. Not just the Thames, but the Fiddlers Island Stream, Castle Mill Stream, Bulstake Stream, Osney Ditch and the Oxford Canal.

88 Street of Three Colleges

Turl and turl again

Turl Street is one of Oxford's most exciting streets, buzzing with business, ablaze with activity. Here, in the centre of the university area, are three colleges: Jesus on the west side, and Exeter and Lincoln on the east.

Jesus College was founded in 1571 by Queen Elizabeth, and was so named because her regime, being Protestant, venerated the Son rather than the Catholics' Virgin Mary. It's not surprising students refer to it simply as Jesus, for its official name is '*Collegium Jesus infra civitatem et Universitatem Oxoniae ex fundatione Reginae Elizabethae, Anglice vero* – Jesus College wythin the Citie and Universitie of Oxforth, of Quene Elizbethe's fundacion'.

Jesus' two greatest alumni are both 20th-century heroes: T. E. Lawrence was a military winner in the Great War and a ferociously realist writer. Harold Wilson, Labour prime minister a joint record four times, was a rare politician who achieved major new social advances, including the decriminalisation of homosexuality. Exeter College is Alma Mater of William Morris the Victorian aesthete; Tolkien; and the wit Alan Bennett.

It was in the wars in 2018 when a mob of 200 students stripped and trashed the college chapel during a booze-fuelled party. Lincoln College was John Wesley's. According to Pevsner, it preserves 'more of the character of a 15th-century college than any other in Oxford'. Its own Freshers' handbook boasts that 'unlike most colleges, we have no grotty sixties annexe to spoil all the pretty bits'.

Turl Street was originally St Mildred's Street, but was renamed Turl Gate Street in the mid-17th century in honour of a twirling gate that was demolished in 1722. Its history is full of religious jokes. An American tourist entered Lincoln College one day and asked the porter: 'Say buddy, is this Jesus?', to which the porter replied: 'Typical Yank; thinks Lincoln was Jesus'.

Address Turl Street OX1 3DQ, www.jesus.ox.ac.uk, www.exeter.ox.ac.uk, www.lincoln.ox.ac.uk | **Getting there** Bus 3, 3A, 6 or 8; a 10- to 15-minute walk east from Oxford Station | **Hours** Outside accessible 24 hours. Jesus College is only open to pre-booked groups; Exeter College is currently closed to visitors; Lincoln College welcomes visitors Mon–Fri 2–5pm, Sat & Sun 11am–5pm | **Tip** After visiting three top rank colleges, possibly in one go, you will need a stiff drink, procurable at the Whisky Shop at Number 7 (www.whiskyshop.com).

89 Suffragette Bomb House
Spirits in the material world

July 1912: suffragettes Norah Smyth and Helen Craggs hire a boat and row up the Thames so that they can set fire to this 18th-century Palladian-style villa. You can see their point. It was home to Lewis Harcourt, a Liberal MP who opposed women having the vote. Nuneham House, now the Brahma Kumaris World Spiritual University and Global Retreat Centre, was built in 1756. The original owner, Lord Harcourt, didn't endear himself to locals by demolishing the entire ancient village of Nuneham Courtenay to create the estate, even if the new grounds were designed by Capability Brown. He even diverted the Oxford to London road. The destruction was captured for all time in literary form in Oliver Goldsmith's poem *The Deserted Village* (1770).

In 1904, Sir William Harcourt unexpectedly inherited Nuneham, which by then was in a dilapidated state. When he told his agent 'I appear to have inherited a bankrupt estate', the latter replied, 'And whose fault do you think that is, Sir William?', reminding the aristo that it was he as Chancellor of the Exchequer who had introduced death duties in 1894. Sir William died shortly after, possibly from the shock, and the house passed to his son, Lewis, one of the leading Parliamentarians to speak out against the suffragettes. That's why, in the early hours of 13 July, 1912, Smyth and Craggs attacked. But their plan to burn the house down failed when they were apprehended by a PC Godden. Craggs was arrested; Smyth fled, rowed to Abingdon, made her way to Reading, where she changed her clothes, and crossed the Channel till the dust settled.

During World War II, the Ministry of Defence requisitioned the estate and it became RAF Nuneham Park. It was used until 1957 as the Central Interpretation Unit for Air Surveillance Photography and later sold to Oxford University as a hall of residence, until it took up its current role.

Address Nuneham Estate, Nuneham Courtenay OX44 9PG, +44 (0)1865 343413 | Getting there By car, take the A 4074 and head west at the signs for Nuneham Courtenay | Hours Viewable from the road only | Tip In the grounds is the original elaborate and ornate Carfax conduit that supplied water to the middle of Oxford.

90 Sundial at All Souls
Time has come today

'And where round the sundial / The reluctant hours of day,
   Heartless, hopeless of their way, Rest and call.'
'Love's Nocturn' – Dante Gabriel Rossetti (1854)

Of all the sundials across Oxford, All Souls' 1658 model is the most magnificent. It is decorated with a cartouche of the college arms and topped with a cornice of a cherub. The Latin inscription at the foot of the dial reads *Pereunt et imputantur* – 'The hours pass away and are counted against us'.

Sundials were the earliest form of timekeepers. Although it is not certain that Christopher Wren was this one's designer, Pevsner notes in his *Buildings of England* series that 'As Christopher Wren was Bursar that year, it is a reasonable assumption that he designed it'. Indeed, few people at that time had the ingenuity to create something so complex. Wren had an interest in sundials from an early age. John Aubrey in *Brief Lives* wrote of how when Wren was in his teens, he made 'severall curious Dialls, with his owne handes'. At Oxford, Wren also designed a box-beehive, a hygrometer to measure the amount of water vapour in the air, and an instrument for writing two copies of a document at the same time. He and John Wilkins built an 80-foot telescope to observe the Moon.

Until the beginning of the railways, which needed set time, and the later invention of the telegraph, which meant people could instantly discover that there were different times east–west across the world, sundials were more than merely decorative. They were the means by which people set clocks and watches. The All Souls sundial was moved in 1877 from the south wall of the college chapel to its current location outside the library. John Simmons, a recent Fellow, campaigned to have it restored to its original position. Before he died in 2005, Simmons left a bequest of £888,000 to the college with this condition attached. The college wasn't keen.

Address High Street, just east of Catte Street OX1 4AL, +44 (0)1865 279379, www.asc.ox.ac.uk | Getting there Bus 3, 3A, 8 or 10; a 20-minute walk from Oxford Station | Hours Mon–Fri 2–4pm, Sun when the college is open, so check with the Porters' Lodge before visiting | Tip Take in a service at All Souls' college chapel, a now rare establishment that uses the Book of Common Prayer and the King James Bible, rather than one of those new-fangled trendy happy-clappy versions in Scouse or summat.

91 The Supergrass Pub

In it for more than the money

Imagine a group that combined the melodic spirit of the Beatles, the spark of the Rolling Stones, the cheek of the Sex Pistols and the dynamics of Led Zeppelin. Yes, yes, the Smiths, but also Supergrass. Formed in Oxford by over-confident school-leavers Gaz Coombes and Danny Goffey, joined by Mick Quinn, they secured a record deal after performing a gig here, the Jericho Tavern, in 1994. Supergrass soon caused a splash with the amusing autobiographical single 'Caught By The Fuzz', which recounted the singer's experience of being arrested by the peelers for smoking da weed and having to explain his predicament to his mum. With great irony thieves, as if trying to re-create the tenor of the single, later tried to steal a plaque honouring the group's sojourn. Unlike in the song, the robbers were not caught by the fuzz.

A run of ballsy, brazen, adolescent romps led to a cracking 1995 debut album in *I Should Coco*, which sold more than a million copies worldwide. Even then, no one was prepared for the majesty of their second LP, *In It For The Money* (1997), a glorious amalgam of '60s psychedelia, '70s punk and '80s production polish. The Small Faces reborn.

The Jericho Tavern is now a major music pub. Apart from Supergrass, it's witnessed Mumford and Sons, Pulp, and the Bombay Bicycle Club (not from Bombay; not necessarily cyclists). The pub dates back to the 17th century, when people coming to Oxford after the city gates had shut could take refuge in what was then the Jericho House. It was rebuilt in 1818, sadly became a Berni Inn in the 1960s, and in 1984 featured a women-only bar, until the landlord closed it down when he found customers smoking da weed again, and kissing! By the mid-1990s, during the mania for pubs with unfunny Firkin appellations, it was the Philanderer and Firkin. Could it get worse? Yes. Radiohead made their debut here in 1987.

Address 56 Walton Street OX2 6AE, +44 (0)1865 311775, www.thejerichooxford.co.uk |
Getting there Bus 6; a 10-minute walk from Oxford Station | **Hours** Sun–Thu noon–11pm,
Fri & Sat noon–midnight | **Tip** Finished supping at the Jericho Tavern? Cross the road to
the Victoria – real ale, real fire, simple pub food (www.victoriapub.co.uk).

92 Swinford 5p Toll Bridge

For whom the bridge tolls

Tolls for pedestrians were abolished in 1835, but there are still punitive charges for cars crossing the Thames just above Eynsham Lock between Eynsham and Swinford – five pence. In a hostile blow to the local financers this was an increase from what it had been until 1994 when it was two pence a car.

Swinford Toll Bridge, privately owned, carries the B4044. It is Grade II listed, and a scheduled ancient monument. The bridge was built because at Swinford the Thames unusually runs in a single channel, the ancient ferry could not take carriages, and the river often flooded. In 1755, the local landed gentry decided to upgrade the local turnpike roads and build a limestone bridge, funded by the Earl of Abingdon, and it opened in 1769. This was a massive help in the fight against highwaymen, who would lurk by the bank waiting for ferry users. At the same time, laws were passed to make the building of more bridges across the river illegal for three miles. They cited a ruling passed with the Magna Carta that protected the people from being asked to pay for bridges 'where never any were before', which was why the Earl coughed up.

Turnpikes were one of the central pillars of the Industrial Revolution, vital in ensuring roads were of sufficient quality to transport the newly manufactured goods. By 1836, there were more than 20,000 miles of turnpike roads, and then the railways took over. According to the county council, some 10,000 vehicles cross Swinford Bridge each day, which is a lot of five pences. Can you believe, not everyone pays, but felons are caught by CCTV. A century ago, John Piercy, a yeoman, had to apologise to Lord Abingdon for forcing his way through without shelling out. Meanwhile, a recent *Witney Gazette* poll showed that nearly 90 per cent of locals wanted the tolls scrapped. In 2009, the bridge was put up for sale, and went at auction for £1.08 million.

Address Swinford Bridge, Witney OX29 4BX | Getting there The bridge is part of the B 4044 | Hours Accessible 24 hours | Tip Stay on dry land in Wytham Woods, located just to the east.

93 Tailors to the Posh Boys
Bullingdons in a china shop

Imagine arriving at Oxford University and, never mind studies, being invited to join one of the many private, élitist, secretive drinking and dining clubs: the Gridiron, the Assassins, the Piers Gaveston, the Pythic Club. Of these, the most feared, however, is the Bullingdon. Noisier than Leeds fans, wilder than Millwall, better dressed than Andy Burnham and his Oasis crew, recent initiation ceremonies have included branding a 'B' with hot wax onto new members' arms.

Only the *crème de la crème* make it. Past members include Dave, Boris, Edward VIII and those who should have known better, such as David Dimbleby. Ede & Ravenscroft, Oxford's most famous tailors, who hold royal warrants and serve the king himself, supply the correct *mufti*, which is exact and uncompromising: blue tie, blue coat, brass buttons, buff waistcoat, blue trousers. This will only cost £4,000; or is it £5,000? Not all Bullers are proud of their past antics. In a 2013 documentary, Boris Johnson confessed that he looked back on those days with a sense of 'self-loathing'. When reminded of his exploits he described them as 'a truly shameful vignette of almost superhuman undergraduate arrogance, toffishness and twittishness'.

On the shop wall is a blurred Bullingdon photo from 1925 featuring such revered members as Sir Hugh Vere Huntly Duff Munro-Lucas-Tooth, who became an MP at 21; Roger Lumley, later the Grandmaster of the British Freemasons; and Lord Longford who became Labour leader of the House of Lords and the embarrassing supporter of Moors murderer Myra Hindley. Such figures were expertly sent up by Evelyn Waugh in his first novel, *Decline and Fall* (1928), as 'epileptic royalty from their villas of exile; uncouth peers from crumbling country seats; smooth young men of uncertain tastes from embassies and legations; illiterate lairds from wet granite hovels in the Highlands'.

Address Ede & Ravenscroft, 119 High Street OX1 4BX, +44 (0)1865 242756, www.edeandravenscroft.com | Getting there Bus 3, 3A, 8 or 10; the western end is a 12-minute walk from Oxford Station | Hours Tue–Sat 10am–5pm | Tip If you're not satisfied with Ede & Ravenscroft then you can always nip over to No. 109 and try Shepherd and Woodward.

94_ Thirsty Meeples
Never be board again

Looking for some serious intellectual activity? Pop into Thirsty Meeples where there are just 2,700 board games to choose from while snacking and supping. As John Lydon once sang, 'It's not a game of monopoly', for you can choose such unlikely pursuits as 'Merchant of Venus', 'Paranormal Detectives' and 'Mouse, Cat, Cheese, Cucumber' (what it says on the trap).

A group of enthusiasts began Thirsty Meeples in 2016 as the first of its kind in Britain, hosted by a team of Game Gurus. Heated banter is a constant. Like the time one punter was heard to remonstrate with his friends over a game of Articulate: 'Rat pack singer... nicknamed Ol' Blue Eyes... First name rhymes with Spank!' Ask for the Royal Game of Ur, made of wood and shell, believed to be the oldest game in the world, found in a cemetery in southern Iraq and dating back to 2600 B.C. A British Museum curator deciphered the rules and discovered that two players compete to race their pieces from one end of the board to the other. Along the way, the central squares can be used for fortune telling.

Equally antiquated and legendary is Mehen, named after an Egyptian snake god, dating back to around 2300 B.C. The board is in the shape of a coiled snake, while teams of up to six players race from the tail to the head and back. Unfortunately, the rules and scoring are unknown. Or you can ask for Hyena, a North African game where players race a piece along a spiral track from the village to the centre, the first to finish releasing a hyena, which eats other players' pieces as it goes.

Ingeniously, every fourth Sunday, PlayTest allows customers to bring a new game they've created so that members of the public can play it and give feedback. You pay a cover charge for three hours' play, which is reduced if you buy drinks or eats. If you can't bear to be parted from your choice, you can always buy it of course.

Address 99 Gloucester Green OX1 2DF, +44 (0)1865 244247, www.thirstymeeples.co.uk | **Getting there** Bus 6 or 13; Oxford Station is nearby | **Hours** Mon–Fri 11am–midnight, Sat & Sun 9am–midnight | **Tip** Be properly dressed! Drop into Laird Hatters on Cornmarket for some classic Oxonian headwear.

95 The Ties That Bind Pub

Bear with the landlord's foibles

On the walls and ceiling of the Bear, an ancient inn, possibly the oldest in Oxford, are more than 4,000 ties. This strange phenomenon dates back to the 1950s when landlord Alan Course, a cartoonist for the *Oxford Mail*, started clipping off the end of patrons' neckwear. He insisted that only those bearing the insignia of a particular club, school, police force, military unit could be displayed. Those on show range from the Royal Gloucestershire Hussars and the Imperial Yeomanry to the Punjab Frontier force and Lloyds of London's Croquet club. The ties are displayed in glass-fronted cases attached not just to the walls but to the ceiling as well. Each piece comes with a label denoting the owner with their signature. Originally, the victim earned a free pint, but that custom is no longer observed.

More violent dramas have taken place here. In 1586, Magdalen students attacked the diplomat Lord Norris after some of their number had been imprisoned for poaching deer. Celebrities have flocked here. Elizabeth Taylor and Richard Burton popped in in 1963. Twenty years later, after a session at the Bear, Ian Gillan, the long-haired quasi-operatic vocalist formerly with top-drawer heavy rock outfit Deep Purple, was convinced to join the even greater top-drawer heavy rock outfit Black Sabbath, a move that was far from successful.

In Colin Dexter's Inspector Morse novel *Death is Now My Neighbour*, the sullen 'tec visits the Bear to find evidence. He shows a photograph of a man wearing a maroon tie with a narrow white stripe, hoping to learn which school or club the man had attended: 'A bit like a farmer looking for a lost contact lens in a ploughed field,' only to be told 'You'll find one just like that in the tie rack at Marks and Spencer's.' In another story, Morse chases a prisoner through the bar. This is a traditional pub: no music, fruit machines or TV.

Address 6 Alfred Street OX1 4EH, +44 (0)1865 728164, www.bearoxford.co.uk | Getting there Bus 3, 3A, 8 or 10; a 12-minute walk from Oxford Station | Hours Mon 3–10.30pm, Tue–Sun midday–11pm | Tip Next door to the pub is the highly regarded research firm of Oxford Analytica, not to be confused with Cambridge Analytica, the data firm set up by former Donald Trump advisor Steve Bannon.

96__Tom Tower Bell

How many times?

In some places, a seemingly non-stop peel of bells would be an annoyance. But in Oxford, where a sublime spirituality pervades the air, the city would not be complete without the Great Tom bell at Christ Church dinging and donging no fewer than 101 times – really – every evening around 9pm. And if you think that's strange, it does so not on the hour, but at 9.05pm.

Why five past nine? Because Oxford, historically, traditionally, did not enjoy exactly the same times as London. The great university city is one degree longitude west of the Greenwich Meridian that sets time internationally. So when it is 9pm in the capital, it is technically 8.55pm in Oxford, despite universal time across the British Isles. Accordingly, the nine o'clock bell goes off at five past nine.

Before the coming of the railways in the 1830s, it wasn't important to know that when it was noon in London (when the Sun was at its highest), it wasn't yet noon 56 miles west in Oxford. Once the railways started, such anomalies caused a problem for timetables. It was only when the telegraph was invented a few years later that people knew for certain, for the first time, that everywhere had different times moving east–west. Consequently, time was standardised across the British Isles. However, this is Oxford, so the old traditions remain.

But why 101 times and not just nine to indicate the o'clock? That dates back to a tradition that each ding or dong remembers the original 101 students of Christ Church, the college situated here, warning them to return before the gates were locked. The bell has rung every night since World War II, except for one day in 2002 when it was briefly silenced after a student prank.

Tom Tower, designed by Christopher Wren in the 1680s, is situated over the main entrance of Christ Church, the name by which the college is known, never as Christ Church College.

Address St Aldates, opposite Pembroke Square OX1 1DP | Getting there Bus 1, 5 or 5A;
Oxford Station is 10 minutes to the west | Hours 9.05pm every night | Tip Book a visit to
Christ Church, one of the wonders of not just Oxford but the universe (www.chch.ox.ac.uk).

97 Traffic Bollard From Hell

'Driving in My Car'…or maybe not

Oxford is where the motor car was pioneered by the ingenious William Morris, but killjoys at Oxfordshire County Council HQ want to trap people in their homes by making it impossible to drive a vehicle without invoking punitive fines.

The problem stems from council officials, drunk on the unaccountable power they had during Covid, still desperate to ruin, sorry run, people's lives. At first, it seemed the scheme was sensible: create low traffic neighbourhoods (LTNs), stopping cars and motorcyclists heading through residential streets. However, it didn't take long before the public realised that all it did was move traffic onto the main roads, which became log-jammed. To ensure people kept to the new rules, Oxfordshire fitted bollards. Did the generally law-abiding burghers of the great university accept it all with good grace? Huh! They drove over the bollards, pulled them out of the ground and, on some occasions, sawed them off!

Most of the vigilante activities have taken place here on Howard Street, off the Iffley Road, where the guv'nor bollard has been dubbed 'the most hated in the UK'. It has been set ablaze and replaced with a sturdy wooden post. Humph. Local activist Amir Steve Ali told journalists: 'It's costing the taxpayers thousands of pounds to fix every time as well.

The LTN pushes all the traffic out of Howard Street and onto nearby Cowley Road. There's more congestion and more pollution in Oxford than ever before. The problem has just been moved to another street. It's like chucking your rubbish next door.'

Oxfordshire had spent more than £12,000 replacing the damaged bollards, only for them to be damaged again. Interestingly the County Council is based right next to the ancient Oxford Castle with its cells that long held prisoners dangling from their feet upside down. Who will win this battle? Which side will face such punishment?

Address Howard Street OX4 3AZ | **Getting there** By car, head south along the Cowley Road (B 480), but don't drive. They'll have you! | **Hours** Accessible 24 hours | **Tip** There is some seriously interesting street art in Cowley, including a massive portrait of David Attenborough.

98 Trinity College Gates

Under holy orders and under starter's orders

Through these Trinity gates have wandered some of the most successful figures in British history. William Pitt the Elder was Britain's most powerful politician in the mid 18th-century, during one of the greatest periods of Britain's imperialist expansion. Kenneth Clark became an art expert who devised one of the greatest TV programmes in *Civilisation* in 1969, from the days when the BBC broadcast intellectually stimulating series, as opposed to *Mrs Brown's Boys*. He also sired the irascible Tory politician Alan Clark. Norris McWhirter excelled at athletics in the 1940s, and later became founder and compiler of the *Guinness Book of Records*. It was he who kept the time when Roger Bannister ran the first sub four-minute mile nearby in 1954. However, they don't talk much here about Jeremy Thorpe, 1970s leader of the Liberal Party, whose political and public career descended into ruins when he was charged with planning to murder his gay lover, Norman Scott.

Trinity's full name is 'The College of the Holy and Undivided Trinity in the University of Oxford, of the foundation of Sir Thomas Pope (Knight)'. It was founded in 1555 with a charter that stipulated how all Fellows had to live a monastic existence. Richard Burton, the intrepid 19th-century explorer, hated his time here so much he went to great lengths to get rusticated and was sent down for attending a forbidden race meeting. In 1966, the young Christopher Hitchens, later a leading left-wing intellectual, sprayed across hoardings outside Trinity College the polemical query 'Hey! Hey! LBJ! How many kids did you kill today?', referring to the equally polemical activities in Vietnam of the then American president Lyndon B. Johnson. It is not known whether the graffito had any effect on US policy.

According to legend, the Trinity gates won't be opened until a Stuart sits on the throne of Britain again. Some hopes.

Address Broad Street OX1 3BH, +44 (0)1865 279900, www.trinity.ox.ac.uk | Getting there Bus 6 or 13; a 10-minute walk east from Oxford Station | Hours Currently open at weekends only, 10am–noon & 2–5pm, but it's advisable to call the Porters' Lodge before you visit to check for any updates | Tip Head down the road to George Street and the 1930s Art Deco New Theatre, where you might find anything from comedy stand-up to musicals and gigs of all kinds.

99 The Trout

Get the loot, don't be slow, gonna catch a trout

No glorious summer's day or touristy visit at any time of the year in Oxford can be complete without a visit to this magnificent 17th-century pub. The Trout is perfectly set by an eyot in the Thames, about three miles north of the city centre. Certainly Sebastian agreed in Evelyn Waugh's *Brideshead Revisited* (1945): 'It's half-past five. We'll get to Godstow in time for dinner, drink at the Trout, leave Hardcastle's motor-car and walk back by the river. Wouldn't that be best?' And so have Lewis Carroll, Bill Clinton and even King Hussein of Jordan who have all been seen tippling here.

Victorian visitors would scoff stewed eel washed down with cider cup. No wonder everyone died before they were 50. In Philip Pullman's *Book of Dust* (2017), the inn is home to 11-year-old Malcolm Polstead and his daemon, Asta. C. S. Lewis, of *Narnia* fame, cited the Trout as his second best Oxford pub (after the Eagle and Child on St Giles) and used to dangle his legs over the river wall while eating cheese sandwiches, no less. 'To the Bird and Baby as usual in the morning… then an adjournment to the Trout at Godstow and there drank beer in the sunlight. The beauty of the whole scene was almost theatrical.'

Outside the pub, a colourful peacock called Krug struts on flagstones that were part of the original fisherman's cottage by a narrow wooden bridge that just about looks sturdy enough to contain the weight of an overfed cat. Inside is an extensive menu featuring many dishes using local ingredients (not peacock). The Trout has a ghost of course – Rosamund Clifford, mistress of Henry II, although she is only visible above the knee as the floor level has been raised several times since she went over to the other side. Hence the display of a 1920s poem: 'If I should forget thee, righteous trout, may all my timbers shiver / A port of call to shout about, the best on all the river'.

Address 195 Godstow Road, Wolvercote OX2 8PN, +44 (0)1865 510930, www.thetroutoxford.co.uk | Getting there The pub is near the junction of the A 34 and A 40, although driving spoils the ambience of reaching it on foot two miles up the Oxford Canal from town and then a short distance left along Godstow Road | Hours Mon–Sat noon–11pm, Sun noon–10.30pm | Tip The Perch is the other great Wolvercote pub. It sports a heart-warming, fire-prone thatched roof, flagstone floors and thick stone walls, and it takes a real effort to find, a mile and a half up Binsey Lane off the main Botley Road just west of the station, or a pleasant walk along the Isis (the-perch.co.uk).

100 University College

A brief history of Stephen Hawking's College

Legend surrounds the origins of what might be Oxford's oldest college, an honour also contested by Balliol and Merton. Was University College really founded by King Alfred in 872 or were the papers proving such forged? A less romantic version cites William of Durham in 1249 bequeathing money to support a dozen Masters of Arts studying Divinity.

Within the college buildings is the Shelley Memorial, dedicated to the great early 19th-century poet (1792–1822) who created the perfect sonnet in 'Ozymandias' (1818), which magnificently begins: 'I met a traveller from an antique land/Who said – "Two vast and trunkless legs of stone/Stand in the desert…"'. Shelley arrived at Oxford in 1810 and soon managed to blow up a tree in the courtyard using homemade gunpowder. He was expelled the following year for 'contumaciously refusing to answer questions proposed to [him], and for also repeatedly declining to disavow a publication entitled *The Necessity of Atheism*', according to the College Register. In other words, for writing blasphemous material.

University College overflows with famous alumni. Clement Attlee was the great reforming and nationalising post-war Labour prime minister who created the Welfare State. He read Modern History (1901–04) and according to reports embraced the university lifestyle – rowing, reading and socialising, while a tutor described him as 'level-headed, industrious, dependable, with no brilliance of style'. In complete contrast, Warren Mitchell, ingenious creator of the vile racist TV East End codger Alf Garnett, read Chemistry as an RAF cadet student on a six-month course in 1944. Stephen Hawking gained first-class honours in Physics (1959–62). It was during his final year that he started to experience clumsiness, falling on stairs and having difficulty rowing. At 21 he was diagnosed as having only two years to live, which he managed to defy by 53 years.

Address 88–89 High Street, south side, just east of Magpie Lane OX1 4BH, +44 (0)1865 276602, www.univ.ox.ac.uk | **Getting there** Bus 3, 3A, 8 or 10; the western end is a 12-minute walk from Oxford Station | **Hours** Open 9am–5pm to groups accompanied by a guide (outside term time only) – contact the Visitor Information Point at 44–45 High Street, +44 (0)1865 790522 to book a tour | **Tip** Students and visitors! Start the day with a dollop of Cooper's Oxford Marmalade, and if you forget, there's a plaque to remind you on the wall at 83 High Street.

101 The University's Church

St Mary's – central to English religious history

St Mary the Virgin is the church from which Oxford University grew in the early 13th century. The university was then run from here, lectures took place inside, and degrees were awarded within. And it was here in 1555 that one of the most dramatic and controversial events in English religious history took place: the trial for heresy of the Protestants Hugh Latimer, Nicholas Ridley and Thomas Cranmer. It was fixed that they would be found guilty. They were burned on Broad Street and became known as the Oxford Martyrs. A reminder can be found with a notch cut into the stone on one of the nave pillars that supported a wooden platform during the trial. John Wesley, founder of Methodism, preached here in August 1744, denouncing what he called 'the spiritual apathy' of the university. 'I preached, I suppose, the last time at St Mary's… Be it so; I have fully delivered my soul.' He was never asked again.

Inside are a number of fascinating features. The statue of the Virgin and Child has bullet holes made by Oliver Cromwell's troops. The nave pulpit is where on 14 July, 1833 John Keble gave the sermon that launched the Tractarian or Oxford Movement of clerics who argued for the reinstatement of Christian traditions. In autumn 1939, the writer and academic C. S. Lewis preached a highly influential sermon here, urging people to continue to strive for excellence despite the threat of imminent war. He explained how 'life has always been lived on the edge of a precipice. If men had postponed the search for knowledge and beauty until they were secure, the search would never have begun'.

The Oxford Committee for Famine Relief, made up of Quakers and academics, met in the Old Library of St Mary the Virgin in 1942 and opened their first shop at nearby 17 Broad Street in 1947, later becoming Oxfam (see ch. 37). The view from the top of the church is one of the most sought after in Oxford.

Address High Street OX1 4BJ, just west of Catte Street, +44 (0)1865 279111,
www.universitychurch.ox.ac.uk | Getting there Bus 3, 3A, 8 or 10; the western end is a
12-minute walk from Oxford Station | Hours Mon–Sat 9.30am–5pm, Sun noon–5pm |
Tip Cross the road, head south down Magpie Lane and then into the glorious meadow.

102 Vincent's
Where Jeffrey Archer entertained the Beatles

Vincent's is a posh club – wood panelling, leather Chesterfields, coffee in the best china, not in a paper 'cup for life'. One of its most unusual events took place in March 1964 when the colourful Jeffrey Archer, eventual Tory politician and criminal (no, not for those pulp novels), entertained the Beatles as part of his fund-raising venture for Oxfam. After dropping into Brasenose, they came here for snacks. Ringo was sort of impressed. 'He strikes me as a nice enough fella, but he's the kind of bloke who would bottle your piss and sell it.'

The club was founded in 1863 by the trophy-winning oarsman Walter Bradford Woodgate after he discussed with two rowing friends from Merton their mutual dislike of the Oxford Union. As Woodgate later wrote in his memoirs, 'I swore "hang the Union, I wouldn't be seen there at a dog fight" and was told back: "Well then, when are you going to give us that select club of yours that you have talked so much about?"' As he then explained, 'My dander was up, I called back "This day week"'.

Their first base was above the publishers Vincent's at 90 High Street. One advantage over the Oxford Union was that members were allowed to smoke and drink. Woodgate insisted that Vincent's 'should consist of the picked of the University, selected for all-round qualities; social, physical and intellectual being duly considered'. The club has since attracted the greatest of sportsmen, including four-minute mile runner Roger Bannister and recent gold medal Olympians. Wow, they even started taking women in 2016, but not before 6pm, Tuesday to Friday. And no mobile phones of course.

Shockingly, a photograph of the Beatles standing at the Vincent's bar was stolen from the club in April 2008 after the Varsity Boxing Match. Just don't tell the dons of the 1960s that Oxford now allows students to do dissertations on the Fab Four.

Address 1A King Edward Street OX1 4HS | Getting there Bus 3, 3A, 8 or 10; a 12-minute walk from Oxford Station | Hours Viewable from the street. It's open to members and their guests, so get yourself on the guest list! | Tip Head a few yards south to the junction of Oriel Square and Merton Street to marvel at the extraordinary Canterbury Gate at the back of Oriel College, a Classical wonder with triglyphs, empty niches and fluted pilasters.

103__Walters of Oxford

Where to get your scholarly black gown

Studying the prime minister's course of PPE (Politics, Philosophy and Economics) at Oxford is not like taking a degree in Ice Cream Studies at the University of Cleethorpes. Full academic dress must be worn at all formal university ceremonies, which means popping into Walters for a black gown.

Walters' shop, based in what was an 18th-century coaching inn, has been supplying the nation's undergraduate cream for more than 200 years. This is where you get your *sub fusc* (come on, Latin for dark brown), required when sitting examinations, which has to be worn beneath the academic gown. The rules and regulations take no prisoners:

Dark suit with dark socks, or dark skirt with black tights or stockings. Socks, tights and stockings must be worn (bit tricky) and must cover the ankle entirely. Black shoes. White bow tie, black bow tie, black full-length tie or black ribbon.

There's reams about mortar boards – 'you may remove your mortar board and gown during the examination itself' – phew! There's stuff about religious headwear and army uniforms, but nothing about space helmets. There are even rules regarding the dreaded Covid mask. And here's one that wouldn't impress Sophia Loren: 'When wearing *sub fusc*, your clothing must not leave any part of your legs, ankles, or feet uncovered'. However, at last, a spot of light-heartedness. 'Students traditionally wear carnations for examinations (hooray!) though this is not compulsory (boo).' But even this is wrapped in regulation.

First examination: a white carnation; intermediate examinations: a pink carnation; final examination: a red carnation. All clearly influenced no doubt by the 1957 Marty Robbins hit 'A White Sport Coat and a Pink Carnation'. Alternatively, just sign up to do Ice Cream Studies at Cleethorpes University after all. No sartorial rules other than wearing a pasty-shaped white hat and stripy apron.

Address 10 Turl Street OX1 3DW, +44 (0)1865 241848, www.walters-oxford.co.uk |
Getting there Bus 3, 3A, 6 or 8; a 10- to 15-minute walk east from Oxford Station | Hours
Mon–Sat 10am–6pm | Tip Treat yourself to luxury stationery at Turl Street's Scriptum
amid the smell of leather and the sound of Italian opera (www.scriptum.co.uk).

104 Wasters of Walton Street

Any Piers Gavestons here?

Keep your eyes peeled on Walton Street, Jericho's main drag, especially around summer ball time, for signs of members of the Piers Gaveston Society, the most terrible terrorising tormenting toffs known to mankind.

The club was founded in 1977 and named after the gay lover of Edward II. Past members include actor Hugh Grant, Nat Rothschild and Brexit prime minister David Cameron. Indeed, it is Dave who has been linked with the society's most notorious legend. According to a tale that will be toasted as long as the ale pours out of the spigots in Oxford's beer barrels, during one Piers Gaveston orgy, sorry function, Cameron inserted a priapic piece of his anatomy into a dead pig's mouth as part of the society's initiation ceremony.

Piers Gaveston members address each other by titles such as Lord High Spanker and the High Priest of Pain. They drink themselves senseless while remembering the club motto: 'Fane non memini ne audisse unum alterum ita dilixisse' – 'Truly, none remember hearing of a man enjoying another so much'. The society's orgies, sorry events, are held in the grounds of nearby stately homes, fuelled by vast quantities of drugs to help loosen inhibitions. Female revellers include girls with cut-glass accents wearing in broad daylight, wait for it, 'fishnet tights' (*Daily Mirror*), brightly coloured bodices, PVC hotpants, see-through bras and leather dog collars, being led around by nipple clamps.

But beyond the high jinks and student japes there has been tragedy. In 1986, Count Gottfried von Bismarck woke to find Olivia Channon, daughter of Tory cabinet member Paul, dead in his room after a society event, having choked on her own vomit. Student Lavinia Woodward was spared jail in 2017 despite being found guilty of stabbing her boyfriend with a bread knife while high on alcohol and cocaine from the orgy tent at a Piers Gaveston bash.

Address Walton Street, Jericho OX1 2HD | Getting there Walton Street runs through
the heart of Jericho, the near suburb about a mile north-west of Carfax; bus 6 or S2; a
10-minute walk from Oxford Station | Hours Accessible 24 hours | Tip Walton Street is
all about hardnosed hedonism. It's filled with popular bars and cafés where Oxford's gilded
youth like to unwind.

105 Where Churchill Was Born

By the time they got to Woodstock he'd appeared

Even though he's the best-known British person who's ever existed (apart from the late queen, David Beckham and Ant, or maybe Dec), mystery surrounds exactly in which part of Blenheim Palace Winston Churchill was born prematurely on 30 November, 1874. The latest SP suggests a broom cupboard, not the elegant state room they show you on tours. If you turn to Roy Jenkins' masterly biography of Churchill, the future PM appeared in a 'singularly bleak-looking bedroom', without saying which one. William Manchester is clearer in his trilogy *The Last Lion*. 'Mother Jennie was here dancing at the annual St Andrew's Ball when she was caught out. She stumbled away from the party and lurched past the endless suite of drawing-rooms, through the library, towards her bedroom, but didn't make it. She fainted and was carried into a little room that tonight was the ladies' cloakroom.' Had Churchill been on time, he would have breathed his first in a rented house on Charles Street, Mayfair, the following January. But the London pad wasn't ready, so the family took refuge in Blenheim.

Blenheim is one of the few non-royal or non-religious houses in England to hold the title of palace. It was built in 1705–22 as a reward to John Churchill, First Duke of Marlborough, for his triumphs at the 1704 Battle of Blenheim during the War of Spanish Succession. After construction began in 1705, thanks to a few quid sent by Queen Anne, there was a bit of a barney. With the duke in exile in Europe, the Crown withdrew funds. And if that wasn't bad enough, the architect was Sir John Vanbrugh whose extravagant work was infamously ridiculed by the poet Alexander Pope in the quip: 'Thanks, sir, cried I, 'tis very fine, But where d'ye sleep and where d'ye dine' and whose qualities as a designer were ridiculed by Jonathan Swift 'Van's genius, without thought or lecture / Is hugely turned to architecture'.

Address Woodstock OX20 1UL, +44 (0)1993 810530, www.blenheimpalace.com | Getting there By car, take the A 44 to Woodstock – you can't miss it; train to Oxford Station then bus S 3; bus S 3 or S 7 from Oxford City Centre to Woodstock | Hours Tickets must be pre-booked – see website for complicated opening times. There is a discount on the ticket price if you arrive by train or bus. | Tip Give yourself time to explore the house's infernal maze.

106 White Horse of Uffington

'Prettiest mare I've ever seen'

Pre-history communes with nature at the famous Uffington White Horse. This magnificent hill figure, 120 yards long, was formed from filling deep trenches with crushed white chalk. Its exact birth date is unknown, possibly between 1380 and 550 B.C., which makes it the oldest of the various white horses in Britain, created to celebrate the first uses of the horse in battles. Its earliest reference can be found in medieval Welsh literature, the *Red Book of Hergest*, written between 1375 and 1425: 'Near to the town of Abington there is a mountain with a figure of a stallion upon it, and it is white. Nothing grows upon it'.

Past writers gave it romantic if erroneous origins. Aubrey claimed it was Celtic. Francis Wise in the 18th century claimed it was created by Alfred the Great to celebrate his victory at the Battle of Edington. It was only after an excavation in 1990 that a closer date was established, thanks to the Oxford Archaeological Unit. Until the end of the 19th century, the Uffington white horse was cleaned every seven years. As Francis White wrote in 1736: 'The ceremony of scouring the Horse, from time immemorial, has been solemnized by a numerous concourse of people from all the villages roundabout'. This was usually followed by a festival sponsored by the lord of the manor.

During World War II, the horse was covered with turf and hedge trimmings so that *Luftwaffe* pilots couldn't use it for navigation. In August 2002, it was defaced by members of the Real Countryside Alliance, after which an advert for Channel 4's *Big Brother* TV programme was placed alongside. Then, to embarrass the horse further, as part of a pre-Cheltenham Festival publicity stunt, a bookmaker added a large jockey to the figure. In 2003, the *Guardian* explained that 'for more than 3,000 years, the Uffington White Horse has been jealously guarded as a masterpiece of minimalist art'.

Address Dragon Hill Road, Faringdon SN7 7QJ | Getting there By car, take the B4507 and stop halfway between Compton Beauchamp and Kingston Lisle – you can't miss the horse | Hours Accessible 24 hours | Tip Head east to the town of Wantage and the church of St Peter and St Paul, its bells made famous by the great poet John Betjeman (www.wantageparish.com).

107 — William Morris' Garage
This William Morris, not that one!

Late Victorian and Edwardian eras. What a time to be a cycling or motoring pioneer! And of all those initiates – Karl Benz, Rolls and Royce, Ransom Olds – few were as motivated, as tireless, as successful as William Morris (1877–1963).

This William Morris, not to be confused with William Morris the Victorian polymath who hated cars, taught himself to ride a penny-farthing while still at school. In 1901 he opened a shop at 48 High Street, Oxford, and took over disused livery stables here on Longwall Street, replacing them in 1909 with the Morris Garage, its neo-Georgian façade surviving and now student accommodation for New College. In 1912 he designed his first car, the 'Bullnose', built at a disused military camp in nearby Cowley using components imported from the USA. A year later came the Morris-Oxford Light Car, which sold for £165 and included the noted innovation of a dipstick. Morris pioneered Henry Ford's mass production ideas to increase output from 400 cars in 1919 to more than 50,000 in 1925. Two years later he acquired the prestigious Wolseley Motors and then launched the Morris Minor, unveiled at the 1948 Earls Court Motor Show and designed by Alec Issigonis, who also devised the Mini.

William Morris was a philanthropist, but also a big supporter of the fascist Oswald Mosley. On New Year's Day 1938 he was ennobled as Viscount Nuffield, taking the name of the Oxfordshire village where he lived. Five years later, he set up the Nuffield charitable trust with £10 million 'to improve social well-being by funding research and innovation projects'. This led to the creation of Oxford University's Nuffield College (see ch. 6). But Morris was an unusual character. When he had his appendix removed, he was amazed to receive an anaesthetic, having had a tooth pulled without. How he would despair at today's attack on the car by the authorities.

Address 21 Longwall Street OX1 3SX | **Getting there** Bus 3, 3A, 8 or 10; a 20-minute walk from Oxford Station | **Hours** Viewable from the outside only | **Tip** Hop across the street and find the entrance to visit Magdalen College's Deer Park, home to a herd that has grazed here since 1700, but not the same deer.

108 William Morris' Idyll

Everybody knows this is nowhere

He is one of the most influential designers, aesthetes and intellectuals in English history. Who has never contemplated the excessively ornate decorative wallpaper in a Wetherspoon's pub on the way to the loo and not thought 'bit too much William Morris here'?

William Morris (1834–96) was a painter, printer, medievalist, translator (the Icelandic sagas) and fervent socialist. If only man could return to the honest simplicity and individual craftsmanship of the Middle Ages, Morris mused. He designed textiles, and as an architectural conservationist was the leader of the Arts and Crafts movement, as well as the founder of the Society for the Protection of Ancient Buildings. Morris wrote innumerable unreadable poetry that no one now touches and was a fantasy writer (better), best known for the utopian *News From Nowhere* (1890).

In 1861, Morris founded the firm of Morris, Marshall, Faulkner & Co. with fellow aesthetes Edward Burne-Jones and Philip Webb. Their florid ornate designs had a huge impact on interior decoration, until the rise of clinical clean modernism in the 1930s, but have been copied so excessively and artlessly they have become a cliché. In 1871, Morris rented this rural retreat of Kelmscott Manor, built c. 1570, so that his children could have a bolthole away from the pollution of London. He set up a joint tenancy with Pre-Raphaelite artist Dante Gabriel Rossetti, with whom he sort of shared his wife, Jane Burden.

William Morris described Kelmscott as 'heaven on Earth'. It perfectly fitted his manifesto, given that it was a work of true craftsmanship in harmony with the surrounding countryside. It remained his country home till his death. When his daughter May died in 1938 the house was bequeathed to Oxford University. It passed to the Society of Antiquaries in 1962. Morris is buried in the village churchyard in a tomb designed by Webb.

Address Kelmscott Manor, Kelmscott, Lechlade GL7 3HJ, +44 (0)1367 252486, www.sal.org.uk/kelmscott-manor | **Getting there** Head to the village of Kelmscott and then to the Thames – it's difficult to miss the property | **Hours** Apr–Oct Thu–Sat – gardens and grounds open 10.30am–5pm; manor 11am (final admission 4pm); pre-booking for the manor advisable | **Tip** Check out the village hall – the Morris Memorial Hall.

109 William Tyndale Window

Tribute to one of the greatest of Britons

Ingenious, impelling, inspirational, William Tyndale was not only an heroic figure, but also one of the greatest writers in English history, commemorated with this window in his old college. Tyndale was the first person to publish the Bible in English. He began his monumental work in 1515 in his Gloucestershire bedroom when it was illegal to have an English translation of the Scriptures. The Bible was then only available in the original Hebrew and Greek, or the first Latin translations, kept that way so that the priests controlled knowledge of its contents.

To Tyndale this was an élitist stance, contrived 'to keep the world still in darkness, to the intent they might sit in the consciences of the people, through vain superstition and false doctrine, to satisfy their filthy lusts, their proud ambition, and insatiable covetousness, and to exalt their own honour... above God himself'. He wanted the Bible to be accessible to everyone, so that the plough boy 'would know more of Scripture than the Pope'. Thomas More, Henry VIII's chancellor, was outraged, and denounced Tyndale as a 'beast' and a 'hell-hound in the kennel of the devil'. Tyndale had to go to Germany to get his Bible published and then exported to Britain where, ironically his best customers were the king's men who bought many copies to burn them outside St Paul's.

Tyndale's translations and neologisms were remarkable. Melvyn Bragg has claimed that Tyndale created more popular phrases than anyone before or since: 'An eye for an eye, a tooth for a tooth... Let there be light... The land of the living... The apple of his eye... Go the extra mile'. But Tyndale was hunted down by Papists who opposed the Reformation and imprisoned him in Vilvoorde Castle near Brussels. On 6 October, 1536, he was strangled and burned at the stake in the courtyard. His dying words: 'Oh Lord, open the King of England's eyes!'

Address Hertford College, Holywell Street at Catte Street OX1 3BW, +44 (0)1865 279400, www.hertford.ox.ac.uk | **Getting there** Bus 3, 3A, 8 or 10; a 20-minute walk from Oxford Station | **Hours** Daily 2–4.30pm | **Tip** Book a visit to Hertford that includes the college library. It has an original copy of Thomas Hobbes' *Leviathan*, which he wrote here in 1651.

110 World's Cleverest College
Quod erat demonstrandum

Stand outside the lengthy façade of All Souls College on High Street, just east of Catte Street, and marvel that inside this institution is the greatest concentration of super brains in the world, possibly the universe.

Officially, All Souls is the College of All Souls of the Faithful Departed of Oxford. It was founded in 1438 and is unique in having Fellows and no undergraduates. All Souls is so exclusive, entrance is restricted to just one or two students a year from the 80 or so who apply, and they must already have a Masters Degree. The entrance exam has often been described as the 'world's hardest test'. It's impossible to revise for, as there are no right or wrong answers. No longer though are there one-word questions in the exam such as 'water', 'style', 'innocence' and 'conversion'. Instead, a typical paper might now have 30 questions, from which candidates have to answer three successfully to become life Fellows. Examples include: Should you be allowed internet access during this exam? Is hip-hop/rap more political than the Eurovision Song Contest? Is Edward Snowden a hero or a villain?

Those were easy. What stumped the candidates was 'When will Tottenham Hotspur win the Premier League?'.

Alumni include the leading architect Christopher Wren (1653) and T. E. Lawrence (1919), the military legend forever beatified in one of the greatest of all British films, *Lawrence of Arabia*. Despite all this intellectual rigour, All Souls is also known for its Mallard Song. It's part of a ceremony in which the Fellows process with flaming torches, carrying Lord Mallard seated in a chair, and someone carrying a wooden duck tied to a pole (if they can't find a dead duck). It dates back to the founding of the college, when a giant mallard apparently flew away from the building's foundation. Fortunately it only happens once a century. The last Mallard Day was in 2001.

Address High Street OX1 4AL, immediately east of Catte Street, +44 (0)1865 279379, www.asc.ox.ac.uk | Getting there Bus 3, 3A, 8 or 10; the western end is a 12-minute walk from Oxford Station | Hours College front, quadrangles and chapel open to the public daily 2–4pm (but subject to seasonal closure, so check with the Porters' Lodge or website before visiting) | Tip For further intellectual rigour, cross the road and head for Hoyle's games shop, an emporium overflowing with everything from marbles to Mah Jong (www.hoylesoxford.com).

111 World's Cleverest Street
Merton Street – 'scorchio!'

Bill Bryson called Merton Street 'an architectural treasure-house, one of the densest assemblies of historic buildings in the world'. Here, just off High Street, are the buildings of three colleges: the back of Oriel, and the front of Corpus Christi and Merton itself. Famous past residents include the Great War poet Siegfried Sassoon, who took rooms at No. 14 in 1919, and Tolkien in the early 1970s. Cars are scarce because the street doesn't really go anywhere and because of the cobbles, which the council occasionally ruin by taking them up and replacing them with tarmac.

Merton is one of Oxford's oldest colleges. Legendary alumni include the greatest poet of the 20th century, T. S. Eliot, who was a philosophy postgrad, and the leading historian of Hitler, Ian Kershaw. It's one of the wealthiest; just £298 million the last time the bank account was examined. It's also a hard-drinking joint. To gain admittance into the all-male L'Ancien Régime club, applicants have to tipple from a two-litre bottle of cider with vodka mixer followed by, shockingly, a mandatory dessert of a pack of Ryvitas. Such initiation ceremonies leave college rooms, according to witnesses, 'swimming in sick'.

Corpus Christi is famous for its annual tortoise derby and a recent cookery book, which contains recipes helpful for hard-up students of cocatrice (pig and chicken), stewed oysters, croustades, and lamprey with blood sauce. But its serious importance within the history of Britain is paramount. For it was college president John Rainolds who presided over the creation of the King James Bible, one of the world's most glorious literary treasures. Has this record of intellectual rigour been maintained into the present day? Well, two recent alumni include not only David Miliband, head of International Rescue (no, not *Thunderbirds*), but also his bacon sandwich-eating brother, Ed.

Address Merton Street OX1 4JD | Getting there Bus 3, 3A, 8 or 10; a 12-minute walk from Oxford Station | Hours Accessible 24 hours | Tip Think about attending a public lecture on this street at the Philosophy Centre.

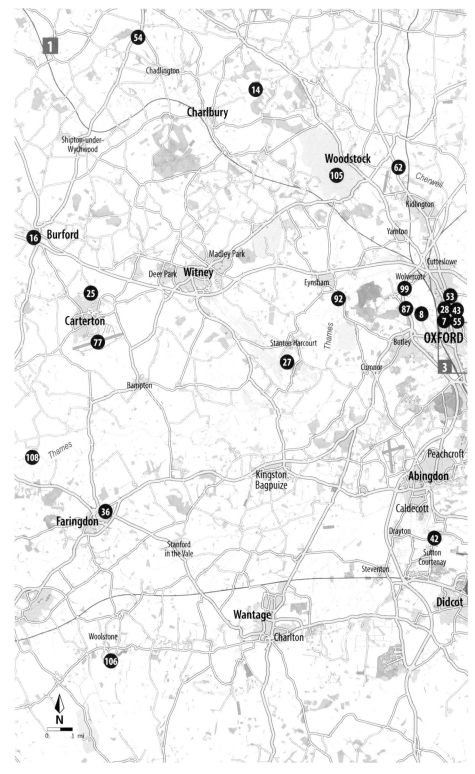

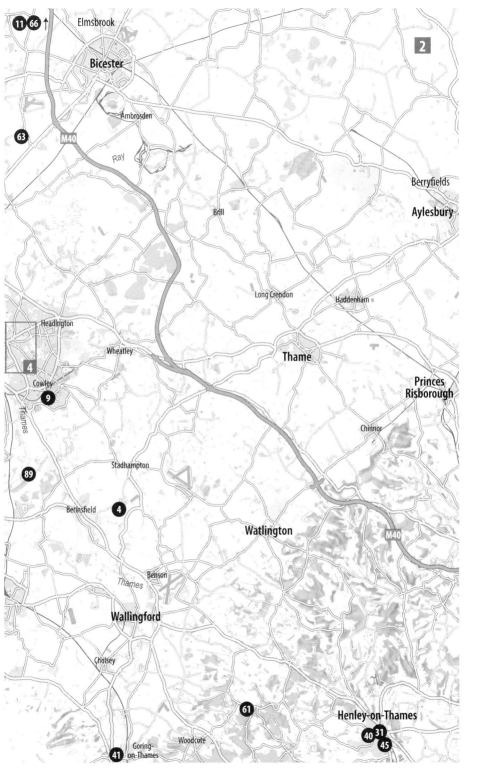

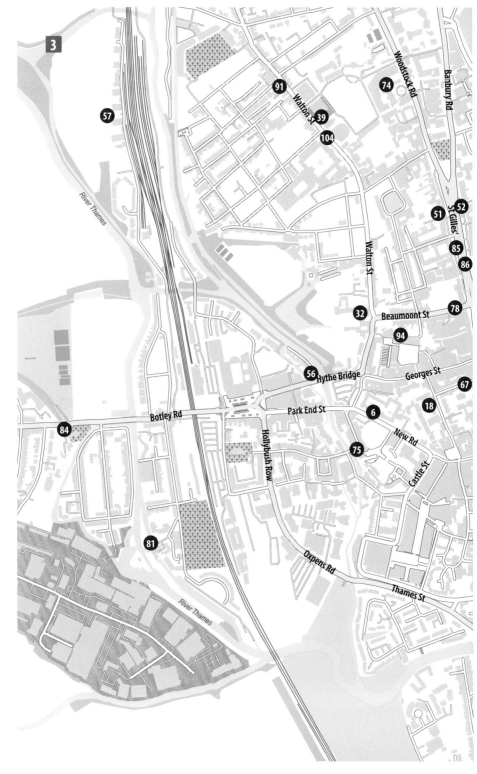

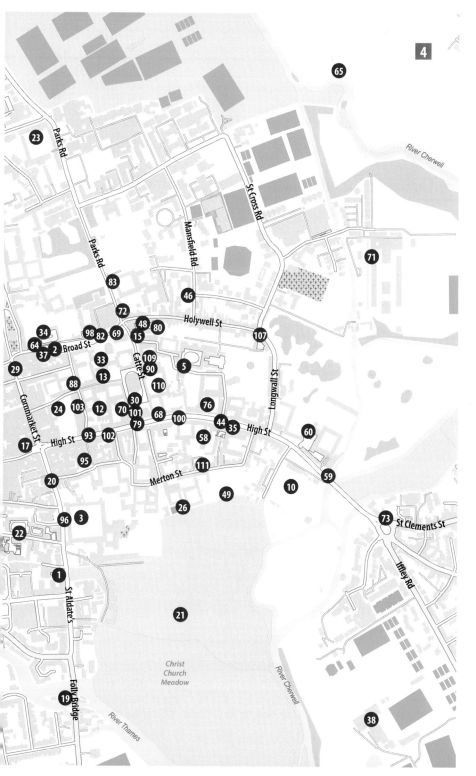

Ed Glinert, David Taylor
111 Places in Yorkshire
That You Shouldn't Miss
ISBN 978-3-7408-1167-9

Ed Glinert, Karin Tearle
111 Places in Essex
That You Shouldn't Miss
ISBN 978-3-7408-1593-6

Ed Glinert, Marc Zakian
111 Places in London's East
End That You Shouldn't Miss
ISBN 978-3-7408-0752-8

Solange Berchemin,
Martin Dunford, Karin Tearle
111 Places in Greenwich
That You Shouldn't Miss
ISBN 978-3-7408-1107-5

John Sykes, Birgit Weber
111 Places in London
That You Shouldn't Miss
ISBN 978-3-7408-1644-5

David Taylor
111 Places in Newcastle
That You Shouldn't Miss
ISBN 978-3-7408-1043-6

David Taylor
111 Places in Northumberland
That You Shouldn't Miss
ISBN 978-3-7408-1792-3

David Taylor
111 Places along Hadrian's
Wall That You Shouldn't Miss
ISBN 978-3-7408-1425-0

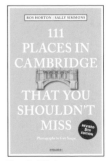

Rosalind Horton,
Sally Simmons, Guy Snape
111 Places in Cambridge
That You Shouldn't Miss
ISBN 978-3-7408-1285-0

Phil Lee, Rachel Ghent
111 Places in Nottingham
That You Shouldn't Miss
ISBN 978-3-7408-1814-2

Ben Waddington, Janet Hart
111 Places in Birmingham
That You Shouldn't Miss
ISBN 978-3-7408-1350-5

Solange Berchemin
111 Places in the Lake District
That You Shouldn't Miss
ISBN 978-3-7408-1861-6

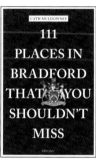

Cath Muldowney
111 Places in Bradford
That You Shouldn't Miss
ISBN 978-3-7408-1427-4

Kim Revill, Alesh Compton
111 Places in Leeds
That You Shouldn∢t Miss
ISBN 978-3-7408-0754-2

Michael Glover,
Richard Anderson
111 Places in Sheffield
That You Shouldn∢t Miss
ISBN 978-3-7408-1728-2

Julian Treuherz,
Peter de Figueiredo
111 Places in Manchester
That You Shouldn∢t Miss
ISBN 978-3-7408- 1862-3

Julian Treuherz,
Peter de Figueiredo
111 Places in Liverpool
That You Shouldn't Miss
ISBN 978-3-7408-1607-0

Katherine Bebo, Oliver Smith
111 Places in Poole
That You Shouldn∢t Miss
ISBN 978-3-7408-0598-2

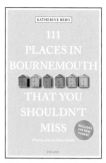

Katherine Bebo, Oliver Smith
111 Places in Bournemouth
That You Shouldn‹t Miss
ISBN 978-3-7408-1166-2

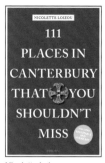

Nicolette Loizou
111 Places in Canterbury
That You Shouldn't Miss
ISBN 978-3-7408-0899-0

Rob Ganley, Ian Williams
111 Places in Coventry
That You Shouldn't Miss
ISBN 978-3-7408-1044-3

Martin Booth, Barbara Evripidou
111 Places in Bristol
That You Shouldn‹t Miss
ISBN 978-3-7408-2001-5

Martin Booth, Barbara Evripidou
111 Places for Kids in Bristol
That You Shouldn‹t Miss
ISBN 978-3-7408-1665-0

Alexandra Loske
111 Places in Brighton and
Lewes That You Shouldn't Miss
ISBN 978-3-7408-1727-5

Justin Postlethwaite
111 Places in Bath
That You Shouldn't Miss
ISBN 978-3-7408-0146-5

Gillian Tait
111 Places in Edinburgh
That You Shouldn't Miss
ISBN 978-3-7408-1476-2

Tom Shields, Gillian Tait
111 Places in Glasgow
That You Shouldn't Miss
ISBN 978-3-7408-1863-0

This book is a team effort, so endless thanks to Laura Olk at the Emons office who gave the go-ahead; Ros Horton, who translated my words into readable English; and David Taylor, once again, for an astonishing array of photographs. Then there are the indispensable friends and relations: Patti-Pea, Katy Walsh Glinert, John Breslin, Sue Grimditch, Jonathan Hill, Michael Hutchison, Emma Marigliano, Juliet Rose, Simon Rose, David Stone, Haidee Tattersall, and last but not least, Lindsay Sutton for listening to the many extracts and laughing at the appropriate places.
Ed Glinert

Shooting the photos for this book would have been more difficult without the help and advice of the following: Samantha Vaughn at Blenheim Palace; Amanda Stinton at Kelmscott Manor; Lisa Venables and Martin Neale at Walters of Oxford; The Reverend Anthony Buckley, Myriam Burstow and Rachael Peace at St Michael at the North Gate Church; Otty Rappoldi at Freud's; Reverend Rachel Cross at St Frideswide's Church; Marc Hanson at Thirsty Meeples; Sarah Ockwell at University Church of St Mary the Virgin; James Hill and Sophie Carp at Hertford College; Sue Gibbons at the Aston Martin Museum; Diogo Santos at Iffley Road Sports Centre; Joanna McKerlie at Reavley Chemist; Sarah Budzier and Dawn Saunders at Christ Church; Robbie at The Trout Inn; and Bev and Paul Vanstone at the Turf Tavern. Thank you!
David Taylor

Ed Glinert is Britain's most prolific tour guide, working in London, Manchester and Liverpool. He is a celebrated author (Penguin's *London Compendium*, 2003), cruise ships speaker and Arts Society lecturer. He is a highly experienced journalist who worked for *Private Eye* magazine for more than 10 years. This is his fourth *111 Places* book after London's East End, Yorkshire and Essex.

David Taylor is a professional freelance landscape photographer and writer who now lives in Northumberland. His first camera was a Kodak Instamatic. Since then he's used every type of camera imaginable: from bulky 4x5 film cameras to pocket-sized digital compacts. David has written nearly 40 books about photography, as well as supplying images and articles to both regional and national magazines. He is the author of *111 Places* books on Newcastle, Hadrian's Wall and Northumberland. When David isn't outdoors he can be found at home with his wife, a cat and a worryingly large number of tripods.